Basic Tips and Instructions f[...]

The Original Recycling Project!
Crochet homespun heirlooms. Simply crochet strips of multi-colored fabrics on a large crochet hook to create lovely accents for your home.

Basic Materials.
Assorted 44" wide [...]
pol[...] [...]cotton blends).
(Outgrown clothing and sheets are suitable).
Size Q crochet hook.
Scissors, Safety pins.

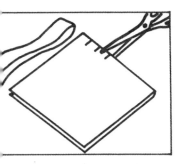

Strips. Fold fabric in half. Clip folded edge. Rip fabric. To join strips, sew, knot or tie ends together. Roll strips into a ball. Optional: Cut fabric with scissors or a rotary cutting tool.

[Jo]ining Strips. Sew [ac]ross ends of strips, if [de]sired. Knot ends and [lea]ve ends free for a [sh]aggy look. Or, cut a [sli]t in the end of each [st]rip. Pull one strip [th]rough slits.

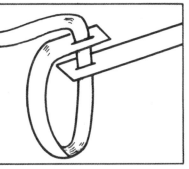

Chain Stitch (ch)
Tie a slip knot in fabric end (this counts as the first ch st). Insert hook though loop. Yarn over hook, pull a loop through (A). Repeat for the desired number of chs (B).

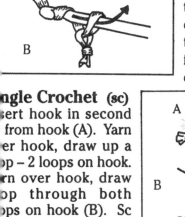

[Si]ngle Crochet (sc)
[In]sert hook in second [st] from hook (A). Yarn [ov]er hook, draw up a [loo]p – 2 loops on hook. [Ya]rn over hook, draw [loo]p through both [loo]ps on hook (B). Sc [co]mpleted (C).

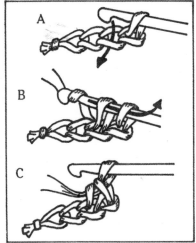

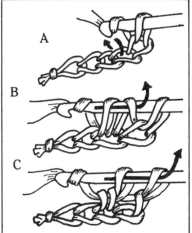

Double Crochet (dc) Yarn over hook, insert hook in 3rd ch from hook (A). Yarn over hook, pull up loop – 3 loops on hook. Yarn over hook, pull through 2 loops (B). Yarn over hook, pull through last 2 loops on hook (C).

Slip Stitch (sl st)
Insert hook in st, yarn over hook, pull up through st and loop on hook.

Changing Colors.
Work last yarn over hook with new color. Pull through last 2 loops of stitch. Lay ends of both colors across top of row and work next several stitches over ends to secure.

Finish Edge. Make increases in stitches at each end to ensure that rug lies flat. If the edge ruffles, too many stitches have been added. Remove some stitches. If the edge pulls under, add more stitches.

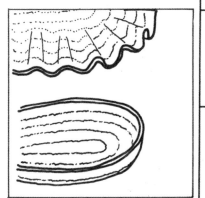

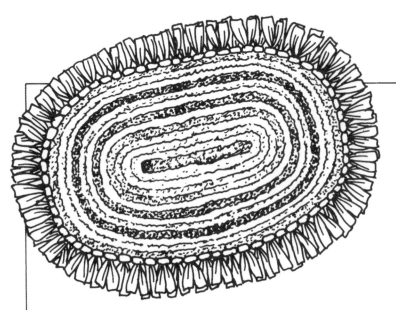

Pastel Oval with Fringe

FRONT COVER PHOTO

FINISHED SIZE: 26" x 38" (including fringe)

GAUGE: 2 sc = 2"

MATERIALS NEEDED: 44" wide Fabric (5$\frac{1}{2}$ yards of Green/Pink print, 2 yards of Dark Green solid, 3$\frac{1}{2}$ yards of Dark blue solid, 3$\frac{3}{4}$ yards of Peach solid, 2$\frac{1}{2}$ yards of Light Green solid - torn into 2$\frac{1}{2}$" wide strips), size Q crochet hook.

INSTRUCTIONS: Chain 20.

Rnd 1 (Pink/Green print): Sc in second ch from hook and in each ch to end. Work 5 sc in last ch. Turn to work across remaining side of foundation chain. Sc in each ch to end. Work 5 sc in loop of turning chain.

Rnd 2 (Dark Green): Sc in each sc to end, work 2 sc in each sc around end. Turn to work across other side, sc to end. Make 2 sc in each sc around end.

Rnds 3-10: Work as for Rnd 2, making increases in stitches at each end to make rug lie flat. Fasten off at the end of Rnd 10.

Rnd 3 (Pink/Green print)
Rnd 4 (Dk. Blue)
Rnd 5 (Pink/Green print)
Rnd 6 (Peach)
Rnd 7 (Dk. Blue)
Rnd 8 (Pink/Green print)
Rnd 9 (Peach)
Rnd 10 (Lt. Green)

Fringe: Cut remaining strips into 7" lengths. working around end of rug, hold 3 strips together. Make a lark's head knot in 1 stitch of last round. Repeat in the next stitch. Use 1 strip to make a knot in the next stitch. Alternate 3-strip knot in 2 stitches, and a single-strip knot in 1 stitch around both ends of rug. Across sides, alternate two 3-strips knots with one 2-strip knot.

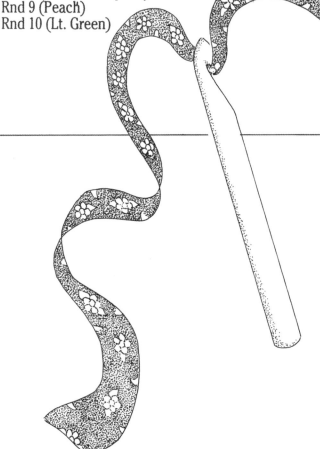

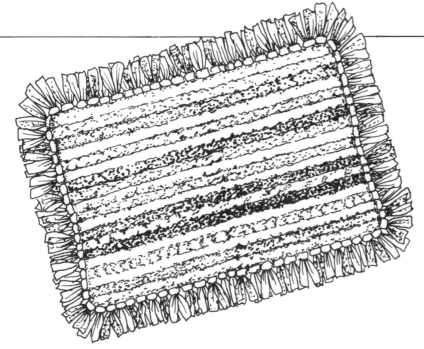

Rectangle with Fringe
FRONT COVER PHOTO

FINISHED SIZE: 22" x 38" (including fringe)

GAUGE: 5 sc = 4"

MATERIALS NEEDED: 44" wide Fabric ($14^{1}/2$ yards of assorted solids and prints- torn into 2" wide strips), size Q crochet hook.

Notes: Work in the back loop of stitches throughout. Rug is worked in rows out from center foundation chain. Change colors for each row. Each row requires approximately $3/4$ yard of fabric. Leave 3" of each strip unworked at each end of each row for fringe.

INSTRUCTIONS: Beginning 3" from end of first strip, chain 51. Fasten off, leaving a 3" tail. This is the center row of the rug.

Row 1: With another color, begin 3" from end of strip, work 2 sc in the first ch, sc in each ch across, work 2 sc in last ch. Fasten off, leaving 3" tail.

Row 2: With another color, begin 3" from end of strip and work 2 sc in back loop of first sc of Row 1, sc in the back loop of each sc across, work 2 sc in the back loop of the last sc. Fasten off, leaving a 3" tail.

Rows 3-10: Work as for Row 2. Turn to work across remaining side of foundation chain.

Rows 11- 20: Repeat Rows 1-10.

Fringe: Cut remaining strips into 7" lengths. Across end, hold 2 strips together and make a lark's head knot in each end stitch of each row. Across side, use 2 strips to make 2 knots in corners. Use 2 strips to make a knot in next st. Make knots with a single strip in each of the next 2 stitches. Alternate 2-strip knots and 1-strip knots in every 2 stitches across.

**Lark's Head Knot -
Fold strip in half. Pull loop up
through a stitch on last row.**

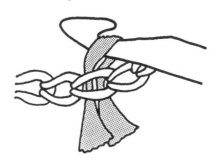

**Pull ends of strip
through
loop.**

**Pull
ends
firmly.**

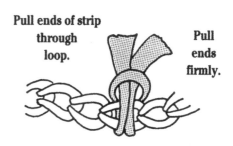

Blue Heart

PAGE 2 PHOTO

FINISHED SIZE: 33" x 24"

GAUGE: 2 sc = 2"

MATERIALS NEEDED: 44" wide Fabric (1 yard of Blue/Green print, $4^1/2$ yards of Lt. Blue, 3 yards of Blue/White print - torn into 2" wide strips), size Q crochet hook.

INSTRUCTIONS: Chain 21.

Rnd 1 (Blue/Green print): Sc in second ch from hook and in each of the next 9 ch. Skip next ch, sc in next ch. (Mark this stitch with a safety pin for center top). Sc in each ch to end. Work 3 sc in last ch. Turn to work across remaining side of foundation chain. Sc in each of the next 9 ch, work 3 sc in next ch. (Mark the center stitch of this group for center bottom). Sc in each ch to end. Work 3 sc in ch - 1 loop at end.

Rnd 2 (Lt. Blue): Sc in each sc to top center st, skip this stitch, sc in next sc. (Move pin to mark this stitch). Sc in each sc to end, work 2 sc in each of the 3 sc around end, sc in each sc to center bottom, work 3 sc in this stitch. (Move pin to mark center stitch). Sc in each sc to end, work 2 sc in each sc around end.

Rnds 3-10: Work as for Rnd 2, skipping the center top stitch, working 3 sc in the center bottom and making increases in stitches at each end to insure that rug lies flat. Fasten off at the end of Rnd 10.

Rnds 3 - 7 (Lt. Blue)

Rnds 8 - 10 (Blue/White print)

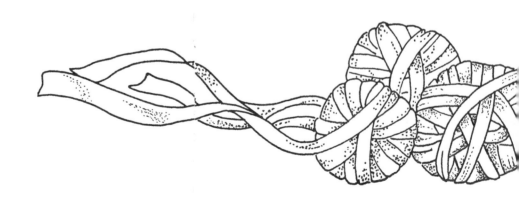

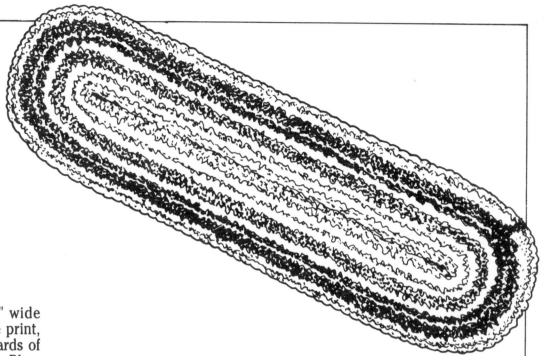

Long Oval Runner

FRONT COVER PHOTO

FINISHED SIZE: 16" x 51"

GAUGE: 3 dc = 2"

MATERIALS NEEDED: 44" wide Fabric (1$1/4$ yards of Blue print, 1$3/4$ yards of Lt. Blue, 2 yards of Orange, 2$3/4$ yards of Dark Blue, 3$1/4$ yards of White, 7$3/4$ yards of Maroon, 4$1/2$ yards of Mauve /White print - torn into 2" wide strips), size Q crochet hook.

INSTRUCTIONS: Chain 50.

Rnd 1 (Blue print): Dc in third ch from hook and in each ch to end. Work 6 dc in last ch. Turn to work across remaining side of foundation chain. Dc in each ch to end. Work 6 dc in loop of turning chain.

Rnd 2 (Lt. Blue): Ch 2, dc in each dc to end, work 2 dc in each dc around end. Turn to work across other side and dc in each dc to end. Work 3 dc in each dc around end.

Rnd 3 (Orange): Ch 2, dc in each dc to end, work, 2 dc in next dc, dc in next dc. Alternate 2 dc with next dc, dc in next dc around end. Dc across other side to end. Work 2 dc in next dc, dc in next dc around end as before.

Rnds 4-8: Work as for Rnd 3, making increases in stitches at each end to make rug lie flat. Fasten off at the end of Rnd 8.
Rnd 4 (Dark Blue)
Rnd 5 (White)
Rnds 6 & 7 (Maroon)
Rnd 8 (Mauve/White print)

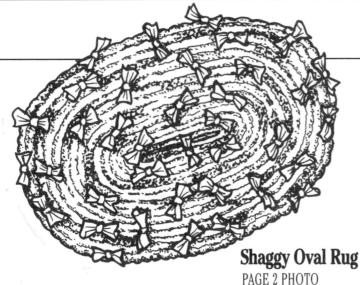

Multi-Color Heart

FRONT COVER PHOTO

FINISHED SIZE: 34" x 31"

GAUGE: 3 sc = 2"

MATERIALS NEEDED: 44" wide Fabric (16 yards of assorted prints and solids - torn into 2" wide strips), size Q crochet hook, 2 safety pins.

Note: Work in the back loop of stitches throughout.

INSTRUCTIONS: Chain 43.

Rnd 1: Sc in second ch from hook and in each of the next 19 chs. Skip 3 ch, sc in next ch. (Mark this stitch with a safety pin for top center). Sc in each of the next 19 ch to end. Work 3 sc in last ch. Turn to work across remaining side of foundation chain. Sc in each of the next 20 ch, work 3 sc in the next ch. (Mark the center stitch of this group for bottom center.) Sc in each ch to end. Work 3 sc in loop of turning chain.

Rnd 2: Ch 1, sc in each sc to within 1 stitch of top center, skip 3 sc, sc in next sc. (Move pin to make this stitch.) Sc in each sc to 3-sc group at end. Work 2 sc in each sc around end. Sc in each sc to bottom center, work 3 sc in this sc. (Move pin to center sc of third group.) Sc in each sc to end, work 2 sc in each sc around end.

Rnd 3-14: Work as for Rnd 2, skipping 3 stitches at the center top on each round and adding stitches at each end and at center bottom. Make increase stitches at each end to make rug lie flat. Fasten off at the end of Rnd 14.

Shaggy Oval Rug

PAGE 2 PHOTO

FINISHED SIZE: 22" x 34".

GAUGE: 2 dc = 2"

MATERIALS NEEDED: 44" wide Fabric (12 yards of assorted prints and solids - torn into 2" wide strips), size Q crochet hook.

Note: To join strips, knot ends together, leaving 2" tails.

INSTRUCTIONS: Chain 11.

Rnd 1: Dc in third ch from hook dc in each ch to end. Work 3 dc in last ch. Turn to work across remaining side of foundation chain. Dc in each ch to end. Work 3 dc in ch-2 loop at end.

Rnd 2: Ch 2, dc in each dc across to end, work 2 dc in each dc around end, turn to work across other side, dc in each dc to end, work 2 dc in each dc around end.

Rnd 3-10: Work as for Rnd 2, making increases in stitches at each end to insure that rug lies flat. Fasten off at the end of Rnd 10.

Long Oval with Shell Border

PAGE 2 PHOTO

FINISHED SIZE: 22" x 46".

GAUGE: 2 sc = 2"

MATERIALS NEEDED: Fabric ($2^1/2$ yards of Lt. Blue, 3 yards of Lt. Blue print, $4^1/2$ yards of White, 4 yards of Medium Blue print, $2^1/4$ yards of yellow, $1^1/2$ yard of Dark Blue - torn into $2^1/2$" wide strips), size Q crochet hook.

Note: Work in the back loop of stitches throughout.

INSTRUCTIONS: Chain 30.

Rnd 1 (Lt. Blue): Sc in second ch from hook and in each ch to end. Work 6 sc in last ch. Turn to work across remaining side of foundation chain. Sc in each ch to end. Work 6 sc in loop of turning chain.

Rnd 2 (Lt. Blue print): Sc in each sc to end, work 2 sc in each of the 6 sc around end. Turn to work across other side and sc to end. Work 2 sc in each sc around end.

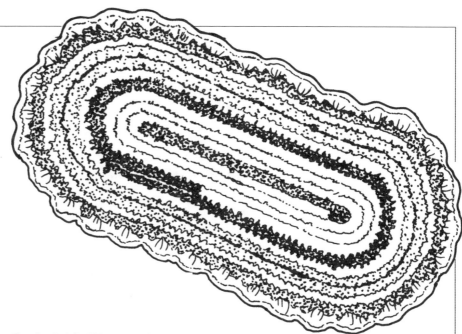

Rnds 3-10: Work as for Rnd 2, making increases in stitches at each end to insure that rug lies flat. There should be an odd number of stitches on the last round. Fasten off at the end of Rnd 10.

Rnds 3 - 4 (Lt. Blue print)
Rnd 5 (Dk. Blue)
Rnd 6 (White)
Rnds 7 - 8 (Medium Blue print)
Rnd 9 (Yellow)
Rnd 10 (Lt. Blue)

Shell Border: (White): Work stitches for border in both loops of stitches on Rnd 10. Attach strip in any stitch of last round, ch 2, work 4 dc in next sc, *skip next sc, sc in next sc, skip next sc, work 5 dc in next sc. Repeat from * around,. End with skip 1 sc, sc in base of beginning ch-2 of border. Fasten off.

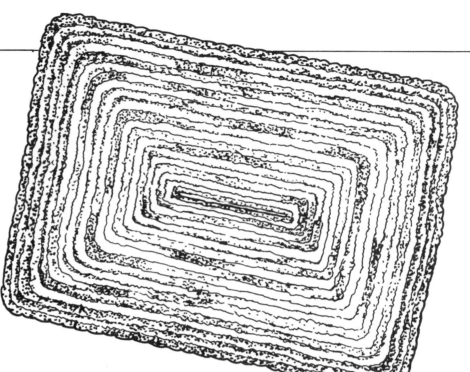

Rectangular Rug

PAGE 2 PHOTO

FINISHED SIZE: 36" x 46".

GAUGE: 3 dc = 3"

MATERIALS NEEDED: 44" wide Fabric (32 yards of assorted prints and solids - torn into 2" wide strips), size Q crochet hook.

INSTRUCTIONS: Chain 12.

Rnd 1: Dc in third ch from hook dc in each ch to end. Work 4 dc in last ch. Turn to work across remaining side of foundation chain. Dc in each ch to end. Work 4 dc in loop of turning chain.

Rnd 2: Dc in each dc to end, work 3 dc in first dc of 4 - dc group at end (corner), dc in each of the 2 center dc, work 3 dc in next dc (corner), dc in each dc across other side to end, work 3 dc in first dc of 4 - dc group at end (corner), dc in each of the 2 center dc, work 3 dc in last dc (corner).

Rnd 3: Dc in each dc across to end, work 3 dc in center dc of next corner, dc in each dc across to center dc of next corner, work 3 dc in center dc of corner, dc in each dc across end, work 3 dc in center dc of last corner, dc in each dc across end, work 3 dc in center dc of last corner.

Rnds 4 - 17: Work as for Rnd 3, making 3 dc in the center dc of each corner group on the previous row.

Rnd 18: Ch 1, sc in each dc around, working 3 sc in the center stitch of each corner group. Fasten off.

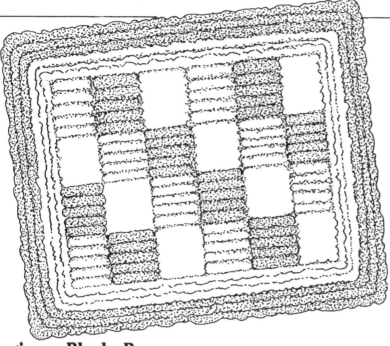

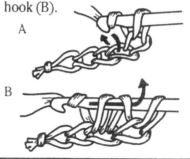

Half Double Crochet (hdc)
Yarn over, insert hook in st or ch (A). Yarn over, pull up loop – 3 loops on hook. Yarn over, pull through all 3 loops on hook (B).

A

B

Beginner Blocks Rug

PAGE 19 PHOTO
Approximate Size of Project: 31" x 38".
CROCHET HOOK: Size **Q**
GAUGE: 2 sc = 2"
Level of Difficulty: Beginner
Additional Materials: Rug needle
STITCHES USED:
Chain st (ch), Slip Stitch (sl st), Single Crochet (sc), Half Double Crochet (hdc), Double Crochet (dc)
Width of FABRIC STRIPS: 2¼" wide (or use 8 Strands of 4-ply worsted weight yarn)

COLOR (fabric or yarn)	FABRIC yardage	FABRIC pounds
Ecru Print	6	1
Med. Blue Print	3	½
Dark Blue Print	9¾	1½

INSTRUCTIONS:
BEGIN Panels 1 & 4: (Make 2) With Medium Blue, ch 6.
Row 1: Work sc in 2nd ch from hook and each ch across - 5 sc. Ch 1, turn. (Note: Mark first row as top of Panel.)
Rows 2-6: Sc in first sc and each sc across - 5 sc. Ch 1 turn. At end of last row, do not ch 1, turn. Attach Ecru in last sc. Fasten off Medium Blue.
Rows 7-12: Sc in first sc and each sc across - 5 sc. Ch 1 turn. At end of last row, do not ch 1, turn. Attach Dark Blue in last sc. Fasten off Ecru. Ch 1, turn.
Rows 13-18: Sc in first sc and each sc across - 5 sc. Ch 1 turn. At end of last row, do not ch 1, turn. Attach Medium Blue in last sc. Fasten off Dark Blue. Chain 1, turn.
Rows 19-24: Sc in first st and each st across - 5 sc. Ch 1 turn. At end of last row, do not ch 1, turn. Fasten off Medium Blue.

Panels 2 & 5: Repeat Rows 1-6 with Dark Blue. Repeat Rows 7-12 with Medium Blue. Repeat Rows 13-18 with Ecru. Repeat Rows 19-24 with Dark Blue.
Panels 3 & 6: Repeat Rows 1-6 with Ecru. Repeat Rows 7-12 with Dark Blue. Repeat Rows 13-18 with Medium Blue. Repeat Rows 19-24 with Ecru.

ASSEMBLY: Whipstitch Panels together as illustrated, with all marked edges at the top.

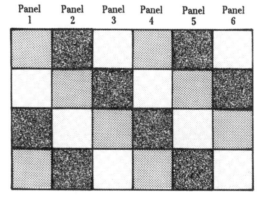

Panel 1	Panel 2	Panel 3	Panel 4	Panel 5	Panel 6

EDGING: Attach Ecru in upper right corner in end of Row 1, just before first st on top row.
Rnd 1: Ch 1, work 3 sc for corner in same space as joining, *sc in next 36 sc, work 3 sc in next row end on side edge for next corner; work 22 sc evenly spaced in row ends across side to last row end, * work 3 sc in last row end for corner. Repeat from* to * around. Join with sl st in top of beginning ch-1.
Rnd 2: Work as for Rnd 1, sc in each sc around, making 3 sc in center of each 3-sc corner group - 136 sc. Join. Attach Dark Blue in last stitch. Fasten off Ecru.
Rnd 3: Ch 1, sc in same sc, 3 sc in next st for corner, sc in each sc around, working 3 sc in center sc of each 3-sc corner group - 144 sc. Join as before.
Rnd 4: Work another row of Dark Blue - 152 sc.
Rnd 5 - Shell Border: Ch 1. *skip 1 sc, all in next sc work hdc, 2 dc, hdc (shell formed). Skip 1 sc, sc in next sc. Repeat from * around to make 38 shells. Sl st to top of beginning ch-1 to join. Fasten off, weave in ends.

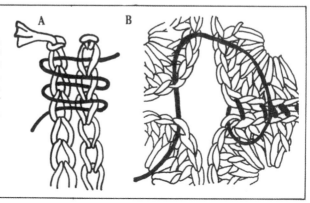

Whipstitch -
With right sides facing, align rows or stitches of pieces to be joined. Insert needle through a back loop of each piece. Insert needle through back loops of next stitches or rows (A). For squares, join center stitches of corners (B).

A   B

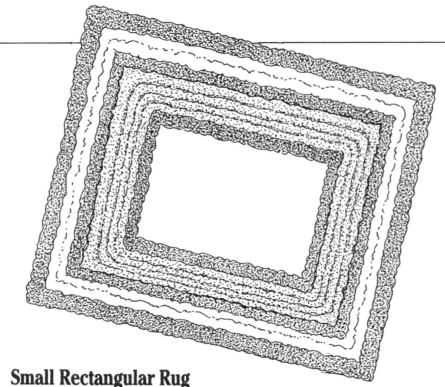

Small Rectangular Rug

PAGE 2 PHOTO
Approximate Size of Project: 23" x 30".
CROCHET HOOK: Size **Q**
GAUGE: 4 sc = 3"
Level of Difficulty: Beginner
Additional Materials: Rug needle
STITCHES USED:
Chain st (ch), Slip Stitch (sl st), Single
Crochet (sc)

Width of FABRIC STRIPS: 2¹/₄" wide
(or use 8 Strands of 4-ply worsted
weight YARN)

COLOR (fabric or yarn)	FABRIC yardage	FABRIC pounds
Tan Print	7	1
Green Print	4³/₄	³/₄
Cranberry Print	3¹/₂	¹/₂

INSTRUCTIONS:
BEGIN: With Tan, ch 15.
Rnd 1: Sc in 2nd ch from hook, sc in each of the next 12 ch, 3 sc in last chain, sc in next 12 ch on the other side of foundation chain, 2 sc in last ch. Join with a sl st.
Rnd 2: Ch 1 (first sc), 2 sc in same stitch as ch-1, sc in next 12 sc, 3 sc in next sc (for corner), sc in next sc, 3 sc in next sc (for corner), sc in the next 12 sc, 3 sc in next sc, (for corner), sc in next sc. Join.
Rnd 3: Ch 1, 3 sc in next sc, *sc in next 14 sc, 3 sc in center sc of corner 3-sc group, sc in next 3 sc, 3 sc in center sc of corner 3-sc group. * Repeat from * to *. Sc in next 2 sc. Join to top of beginning ch-1.
Rnd 4: Ch 1, work 3 sc in next sc, *sc in each sc across to center sc of corner group, work 3 sc in this sc, sc in each sc across to center sc of next corner, work 3 sc in the sc*. Repeat from * to *. Sc in each sc across end.
Rnds 5-8: Work as for Rnd 4 with Tan.
Rnds 9-10: Work as for Rnd 4 with Green.
Rnds 11-13: Work as for Rnd 4 with Cranberry.
Rnd 14: Work as for Rnd 4 with Green.
Rnds 15-16: Work as for Rnd 4 with Tan.
Rnds 17: Work as for Rnd 4 with Green. Fasten off. Weave in end.

Half Double Crochet (hdc)

Yarn over, insert hook in st or ch (A). Yarn over, pull up loop – 3 loops on hook. Yarn over, pull through all 3 loops on hook (B).

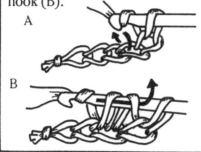

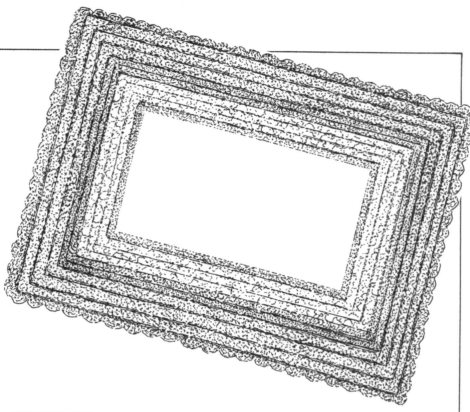

Large Rectangular Rug with Shell Border

PAGE 2 PHOTO

Approximate Size of Project: 44" x 32".
CROCHET HOOK: Size **P**
GAUGE: 3 sc = 2"
Level of Difficulty: Beginner
Additional Materials: Rug needle
STITCHES USED:
Chain st (ch), Slip Stitch (sl st), Single Crochet (sc), Half Double Crochet (hdc), Double Crochet (dc)
Width of FABRIC STRIPS: 1¹/₈" wide (or use 4 Strands of 4-ply worsted weight YARN)

COLOR (fabric or yarn)	FABRIC yardage	FABRIC pounds
Muslin Solid	4¹/₂	³/₄
Red Solid	2¹/₂	¹/₂
Med. Blue Print	1³/₄	¹/₄
Dark Blue Print	3	¹/₂

INSTRUCTIONS:

BEGIN: With Muslin, ch 17.

Rnd 1: Sc in 2nd ch from hook, sc in each of the next 14 ch, 3 sc in last chain, sc in next 14 st across other side of foundation chain, 2 sc in last ch. Join to beginning ch of row.

Rnd 2: Ch 1 (first sc), work 2 sc in same stitch as ch-1, sc in next 15 sc, 3 sc in next sc (for corner), sc in next sc, 3 sc in next sc (for corner), sc in the next 14 sc, 3 sc in next sc, (for corner), sc in next sc. Join.

Rnd 3: Ch 1, work 3 sc in next sc, *sc in each sc across to center sc of corner group, 3 sc in this sc (for corner), sc across to center sc of corner group, 3 sc in sc.* Repeat from * to *. Sc in each sc across end. Join.

Rnds 4-12: Repeat rnd 3, adding 2 sc on sides and ends between corners. Continue to put 3 sc in corners. Fasten off Muslin.

Rnd 13: Work as for Rnd 3 with Red.

Rnds 14-16: Work as for Rnd 3 with Medium Blue print.

Rnds 17-19: Work as for Rnd 3 with Red.

Rnds 20-22: Work as for Rnd 3 with Dark Blue. Do not fasten off.

Shell Border: Ch 1, * sc in next sc, hdc in next sc, work 2 dc in next sc, hdc in next sc*. Repeat * to * around - 50 shells. Work 3 stitches in each corner sc. Join. Fasten off. Weave in end.

Beginner
Granny Square Rugs

PAGE 19 PHOTO:
Pink, Red and Cranberry Rug.
PAGE 2 PHOTO:
Muslin, Tan and Blue Rug.
Approximate Size of Project: 28" x 37".
CROCHET HOOK: Size **P**
GAUGE: each square approximately 9" across.
Level of Difficulty: Beginner
Additional Materials: Rug needle
STITCHES USED:
Chain st (ch), Slip Stitch (sl st), Double Crochet (dc)
Width of FABRIC STRIPS: 1¹/₈" wide
(or use 4 Strands of 4-ply worsted weight YARN)

COLOR (fabric or yarn)	FABRIC yardage	FABRIC pounds
PINK-CRANBERRY RUG:		
Pink Print	5³/₄	1
Cranberry Solid	2³/₄	¹/₂
Red Print	4¹/₄	³/₄
MUSLIN-TAN-PINK RUG:		
Muslin Print	3³/₄	¹/₂
Blue Print	2¹/₄	¹/₂
Tan Print	6³/₄	1

INSTRUCTIONS:
Square: (Make 6) With Pink or Muslin, ch 8 and close into a ring with sl st in first ch.
Note: Ch 3 at the beginning of each round (counts as 1st dc).
Rnd 1: Ch 3, 3 dc in ring, ch 3, work (4 dc in ring, ch 3) 3 times. Join with sl st in top of beginning ch-3. Fasten off.
Rnd 2: Attach Red (or Tan) in any ch-3 loop. (Ch 3, 2 dc, ch 3, 3 dc) in corner loop, dc in next dc, ch 2, skip 2 dc, dc in next dc, *work (3 dc, ch 3, 3 dc) in corner loop, dc in next dc, ch 2, skip 2 dc, dc in next dc*. Repeat from * to * around. Join. Fasten off.
Rnd 3: Attach Cranberry (or Muslin) in any ch-3 corner loop. (Ch 3, 2 dc, ch 3, 3 dc) in corner loop, dc in next dc, ch 2, skip 2 dc, dc in next dc, 2 dc in next space, dc in next dc, ch 2 skip 2 dc, dc in next dc, *(3 dc, ch 3, 3 dc) in corner loop, dc in next dc, ch 2, skip 2 dc, dc in next dc, 2 dc in next space, dc in next dc, ch 2 skip 2 dc, dc in next dc*. Repeat from * to * around., Join. Fasten off.
Assembly: Sew Squares together, matching sts and using the back loop only of each stitch in Rnd 4. Join Squares 3 wide by 2 high.

BORDER: With right side facing, attach Pink (or Tan) in any corner loop of any corner square.
Rnd 1: Work (ch 3, 2 dc, ch 3, 3 dc) in corner loop, *dc in next dc, ch 2, skip 2 dc, dc in next dc, 2 dc in next space, dc in next dc, ch 2, skip 2 dc, dc in next dc, dc in joined corner loop of same square, dc in joined corner loop of next square. Repeat from * to next corner loop, work (3 dc, ch 3, 3 dc) in corner loop. Repeat from * around. Join.
Rnd 2: Ch 5, work (3 dc, ch 3, 3 dc) in corner loop, *dc in next dc, chain 2, skip 2 dc, dc in next dc, work 2 dc in next space. Repeat from * across to corner, dc in next dc, ch 2, skip 2 dc in next dc. Work (3 dc, ch 3, 3 dc) in each outer corner loop. Repeat from * (above) around. Join with sl st to 3rd ch of beginning ch-5.
Rnd 3: Attach Red (or Blue) in corner loop of any corn square. Ch 1, sc in each dc, 2 dc in each ch-2 loop, 5 sc in each ch-3 corner loop around. Join.
Rnd 4: Ch 1, sc in each sc around, working 3 sc in center sc of each corner. Join. Fasten off.

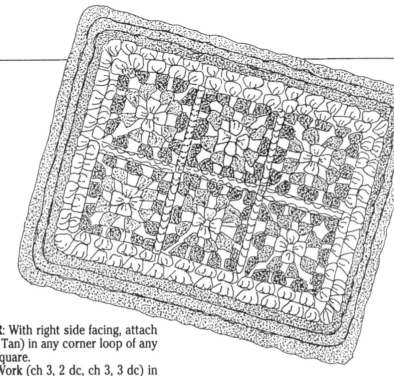

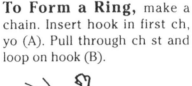

To Form a Ring, make a chain. Insert hook in first ch, yo (A). Pull through ch st and loop on hook (B).

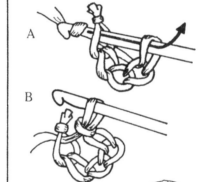

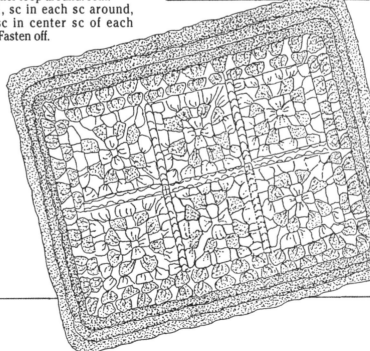

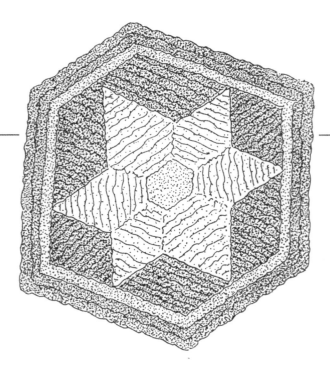

Texas Star Rug

PAGE 2 & PAGE 19 PHOTOS
Approximate Size of Project: 29" across points.
CROCHET HOOK: Size **P**
GAUGE: 3 sc = 2"
Level of Difficulty: Beginner
STITCHES USED:
Chain st (ch), Single Crochet (sc), Slip Stitch (sl st)
Width of FABRIC STRIPS: 1$\frac{1}{8}$" wide (or use 4 Strands of 4-ply worsted weight YARN)

COLOR (fabric or yarn)	FABRIC yardage	FABRIC pounds
Med. Blue Print	1$\frac{1}{4}$	$\frac{1}{4}$
Red Solid	3$\frac{1}{4}$	$\frac{1}{2}$
Dark Blue Print	2$\frac{2}{3}$	$\frac{1}{2}$

INSTRUCTIONS:

BEGIN: With Medium Blue, ch 4. Join to form a ring.
Rnd 1: Ch 1,2 sc in each ch. Join (8 sc).
Rnd 2: Ch 1, 2 sc in each sc around. Join (16 sc).
Rnd 3: Ch 1, *sc in next sc, 2 sc in next sc*. Repeat from * to * around. Join (24 sc).
Rnd 4: Ch 1, *sc in next 3 sc, 2 sc in next sc*. Repeat from * to * around. Join (30 sc). Fasten off Medium Blue.

Star Points:

Row 1: Attach Red in a sc. Ch 1, sc in next 5 sc, ch 1, turn.
Row 2: Sc in next 4 sc, 2 sc in last sc, ch 1, turn (6 sc).
Row 3: Sc in each sc in last sc, 2 sc in last sc. Ch 1, turn*. Repeat from * to * 3 times.(**Rows 4-5**). Ch 1. turn.
Rows 6-13: **Skip 1 sc. Sc in each of next sc across. Ch 1. turn**. Repeat from ** to ** until you have only 1 sc left. Fasten off. (Point made.)

Next 4 Points: To attach, sl st in last sc of Row 1 of previous point. Repeat Rows 1 and 2. At the end of Row 2, sl st in end of Row 2 of previous point.

Repeat Rows 3 and 4. At the end of Row 4, sl st in the end of Row 4 of previous point. Repeat Rows 5-13 to complete point.

Last Point: Attach and repeat Row 1 as for other points. Sl st in the end of Row 1 of first point. Repeat Rows 2-5. Sl st at the end of each row to the end of the same row on adjacent points. Repeat Rows 6-13 to complete point.

Diamond Filler Blocks:

First Block: With right side facing, attach Dark Blue to left side of sc (on Row 13) at tip of any star point.
Row 1: Sc in same space as joining. Sl st in ch-1 loop at end of Row 11 of star point. Ch 1, turn.
Row 2: Work 2 sc in sc. Ch 1, turn.
Row 3: Sc in first sc, 2 sc in next sc. Sl st in ch-1 loop of Row 9 of star point. Ch 1, turn.
Row 4: Sc across to last sc, 2 sc in last sc. Ch 1, turn.
Row 5: Sc across to last sc, 2 sc in last sc. Sl st in next ch-1 loop at end of row of star point. ch 1, turn.
Rows 6-9: Repeat Rows 4 and 5 until there are 9 sc on row. At end of Row 9, sl st in joining st between star points. Sl st in the end of the next row of the **next** star point. Ch 1, turn.
Row 10: Skip 1 sc, sc in each sc to end (8 sc). Ch, 1, turn.
Row 11: Skip 1 sc, sc in each sc to end

(7 sc). Sl st in ch-1 loop at the end of Row 6 of next point, Ch, 1, turn.
Row 12: Work as for Row 10 (6 sc).
Row 13: Work as for Row 11, making sl st in next ch-1loop of point.
Rows 14-18: Work as for Rows 12 and 13 (1 sc remaining). Sl st in right side of sc at tip of next point. Ch 1 over tip, sl st in left side of same sc.
Next 5 Blocks: Repeat Rows 1-13 between each star point. At the end of the last block, join with sl st at right side of sc in star tip, ch 1 over tip, insert hook in beginning ch-1 of first block pull up a loop of Red to complete sl st. Fasten off Dark Blue.

BORDER:

Rnd 1: Ch 1, sc in same space as joining, sc in the end of each row of Filler block to center point (Row 9). Work (sc across ends of rows to next center point, work 3 sc in end of this row) five times around, sc across row ends. Join with sl st in top of beginning ch-1.
Row 2: Ch 1, work (sc in each sc to center sc of 3-sc group at point, work 3 sc in this sc) around, sc in each sc to end. Join. Attach Medium Blue in last stitch. Fasten off. Red.
Row 3: Work as for Row 2. Attach Dark Blue. Fasten off Red.
Rows 4-5: Work as for Row 2. Fasten off. Weave in end.

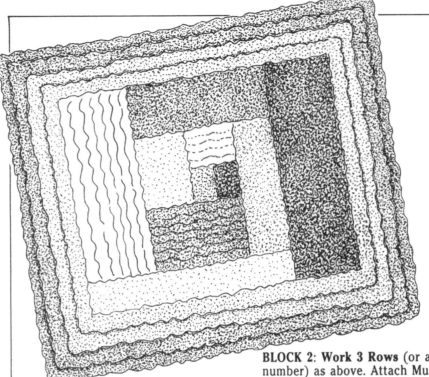

Log Cabin Rug

PAGE 19 PHOTO
Approximate Size of Project: 28" x 22".
CROCHET HOOK: Size **P**
GAUGE: 3 sc = 2"
Level of Difficulty: Beginner
STITCHES USED:
Chain st (ch), Slip Stitch (sl st), Single Crochet (sc)
Width of FABRIC STRIPS: 1 1/8" wide (or use 4 Strands of 4-ply worsted weight YARN)

COLOR (fabric or yarn)	FABRIC yardage	FABRIC pounds

Rug can easily be made from scraps of fabric.

COLOR	FABRIC yardage	FABRIC pounds
Muslin Solid	1 1/4	1/4
Red Solid	2/3	1/4
Dark Blue Print	2/3	1/4
Blue/Pink Print	1	1/4
Tan Print	1/2	1/4
Green Print	1/3	1/4

Note: Instructions are given for rug shown on cover. Feel free to work as many rows for each block as desired. Work either an **odd** or **even** number of rows for each color block according to instructions to change colors. Turn rug and work blocks from center without sewing.

INSTRUCTIONS:
BEGIN: With Red, ch 6.
Row 1: Sc in second ch from hook, sc in next 4 ch, ch 1, turn.
Row 2-4: Sc in each sc across. Ch 1, turn at the end of each row. Attach Blue/Pink in last stitch of Row 4. Fasten off Red. Ch 1, turn.

BLOCK 2: Work 3 Rows (or an odd number) as above. Attach Muslin in last stitch. Fasten off Pink/Blue. Ch 1, turn to work across sides of blocks.
BLOCK 3: Work 5 Rows:
Row 1: Sc in the end of each row (7 sc). Ch 1, turn.
Row 2-5: Sc in each sc across. Ch 1, turn. Attach Tan in last stitch. Fasten off Muslin. Ch 1, turn to work across ends of Muslin rows.
BLOCK 4: Work 5 Rows:
Row 1: Sc in the end of each Muslin row and across foundation chain of Red block (9 sc). Ch 1, turn.
Rows 2-5: Sc in each sc across. Ch 1, turn. Attach Green print in last stitch. Fasten off Tan. Ch 1, turn to work across ends of rows.
BLOCK 5: Work 7 Rows:
Row 1: Sc in the end of each Tan, Red and Pink/Blue row across (12 sc). Ch 1, turn.
Rows 2-7: Sc in each sc across. Ch 1, turn. Attach Red in last stitch. Fasten off Green. Ch 1, turn to work across ends of rows.

BLOCK 6: Work 7 Rows:
Row 1: Sc in the end of each Green row, across last row of Pink/Blue block, and in the end of each Muslin row. Ch 1, turn.
Rows 2-7: Sc in each sc across. Ch 1, turn. Attach Dark Blue Print in last stitch. Fasten off Red. Ch 1, turn to work across ends of rows.
BLOCK 7: Work 9 Rows:
Row 1: Sc in the end of each Red row, across top of Muslin block, and in end of each Tan row.
Rows 2-9: Sc in each sc across. Ch 1, turn. Attach Muslin in last stitch. Fasten off Dark Blue Print. Ch 1, turn to work across ends of rows.
BLOCK 8: Work 9 Rows:
Row 1: Sc in the end of each Dark Blue row, across Tan block, and in end of each Green row. Ch 1, turn.
Rows 2-9: Sc in each sc across. Ch 1, turn. Attach Tan in last stitch. Fasten off Muslin. Ch 1, turn to work across ends of rows.
BLOCK 9: Work 3 Rows:
Row 1: Sc in the end of each row of Muslin, across Green block, and in end of each Red row. Ch 1, turn.
Rows 2-3: Sc in each sc across. Ch 1, turn. Attach Pink/Blue print in last stitch. Fasten off Tan. Turn to work across ends of rows.
BLOCK 10: Work 9 Rows:
Row 1: Sc in the end of each Tan row, across Red block, and in end of each Dark Blue row. Ch 1, turn.
Rows 2-9: Attach Red in last stitch. Fasten off Pink/Blue Print. Ch 1, turn to work across ends of rows.
BORDER:
Row 1: Work (sc in the end of each row or sc across side, work 3 sc in last row or sc) around. Join with sl st to top of beginning ch-1.
Row 2: Ch 1, work (sc in each sc to center sc of 3-sc corner group, work 3 sc in this sc) around. Join. Attach Green in last stitch. Fasten off Red.
Rows 3-4: Work as for Row 2. Fasten off. Weave in end.

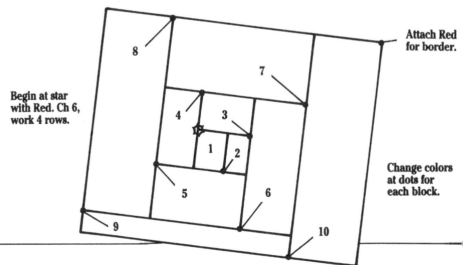

Begin at star with Red. Ch 6, work 4 rows.

Attach Red for border.

Change colors at dots for each block.

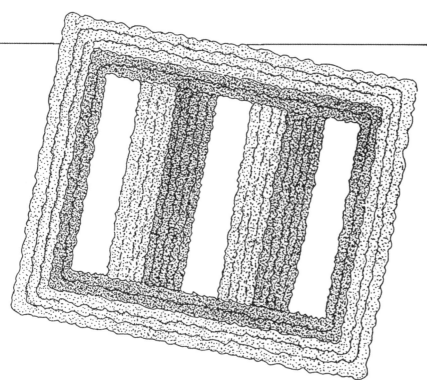

Striped Rug

PAGE 19 PHOTO
Approximate Size of Project: 32" x 36".
CROCHET HOOK: Size **Q**
GAUGE: 2 sc = 2"
Level of Difficulty: Beginner
STITCHES USED:
Chain st (ch), Slip Stitch (sl st), Single Crochet (sc), Half Double Crochet (hdc), Double Crochet (dc)
Width of FABRIC STRIPS: 2¹/₄" wide (or use 8 Strands of 4-ply worsted weight YARN)

COLOR (fabric or yarn)	FABRIC yardage	FABRIC pounds
Tan Print	4	³/₄
Cranberry Print	8²/₃	1¹/₄
Dark Green Print	5	1

Rows 16-20: Repeat Row 2. Attach Cranberry in last stitch. Fasten off Tan.
Rows 21-25: Repeat Row 2. Attach Green in last stitch. Fasten off Cranberry.
Rows 26-30: Repeat Row 2. Attach Tan in last stitch. Fasten off Green.
INSTRUCTIONS:
BEGIN: With Tan, ch 21.
Row 1: Make a sc in the 2nd ch from hook, sc in each of the next 19 ch, ch 1, turn.
Row 2: Sc in each sc across (20 sc), ch 1, turn.
Rows 3-5: Repeat Row 2. Attach Cranberry in last stitch. Fasten off Tan.
Rows 6-10: Repeat Row 2. Attach Green in last stitch. Fasten off Cranberry.
Rows 11-15: Repeat Row 2. Attach Tan in last stitch. Fasten off Green.

Rows 31-35: Repeat Row 2. Fasten off.
BORDER: Attach Green in the first stitch of Row 35. Ch 1, work •(sc in each sc across), 3 sc in the 1st st on the side (for corner), sc in the end of each of the next 33 rows, 3 sc in the end of the row•. Repeat from • to • (118 sc). Join with sl st in top of beginning ch-1.
Rnd 2: Ch 1 (first sc), work sc in each sc across to center sc of 3-sc corner group, work 3 sc in this sc) around. Sc in the last sc. Join. Attach Cranberry. Fasten off Green.
Note: 22 sc across the end, 35 sc across the sides.
Rnd 3-4: Repeat Row 2, adding 2 sc on each side between corners. Do not fasten off.
Shell Border: Ch 1, sc in next sc,* work (hdc in next sc, 2 dc in next sc, hdc in next sc, sc in next sc to corner. Work hdc in first sc of corner group, 3 dc in center sc, hdc in next sc, sc in next sc*. Repeat * to * around - 43 shells. Join. Fasten off. Weave in end.

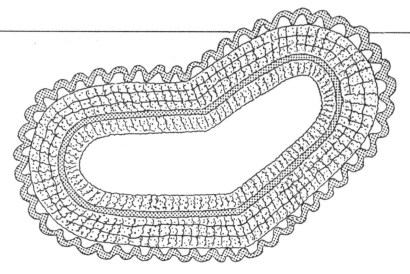

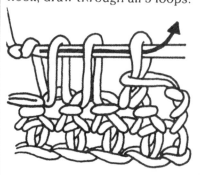

To decrease in sc, insert hook in st, draw up a loop, insert hook in next st, draw up a loop — 3 loops on hook. Yarn over hook, draw through all 3 loops.

Heart Rug with Twisted Loop Border

PAGE 19 PHOTO

Approximate Size of Project: 29" across x 21" high (excluding fringe).
CROCHET HOOK: Size **Q**
GAUGE: 4 sc = 3"
Level of Difficulty: Beginner
Additional Materials: Rug needle
STITCHES USED:
Chain st (ch), Slip Stitch (sl st), Single Crochet (sc)
Width of FABRIC STRIPS: 2¼" wide (or use 4 Strands of 4-ply worsted weight YARN)

COLOR (fabric or yarn)	FABRIC yardage	FABRIC pounds
Muslin Print	2	½
Cranberry Print	2½	½
Floral Print	5	1

INSTRUCTIONS:
BEGIN: With Muslin, ch 22.
Rnd 1: Sc in 2nd ch from hook and in each of the next 9 ch. Skip next ch (dip). Sc in each of the next 9 ch, work 4 sc in last ch. Turn to work across other side of foundation chain. Sc in each of the next 9 ch, make 3 sc in next ch (tip), sc in each of the next 9 sc, work 2 sc in last ch - 46 sc. Join.
Rnd 2: Ch 1, sc in same space as joining, work 2 sc in next sc, sc in each of the next 8 sc, insert hook in next sc, pull up loop, insert hook in next sc, pull up loop, yarn over hook and pull through 3 loops on hook (decrease made), sc in each of the next 8 sc, work 2 sc in each of the the 4 sc around end. Sc in each of the next 10 sc to center sc of 3-sc group at tip. Work 3 sc in this sc. Sc in each of the next 10 sc, work 2 sc in each of the next 2 sc - 55 sc. Join.

Rnd 3: Ch 1, sc in same space as joining, work 2 sc in each of the next 2 sc, sc in each of the next 19 sc, work 2 sc in each of the next 5 sc around end. Sc in each of the next 13 sc, work 3 sc in next sc, sc in each of the next 13 sc, work 2 sc in each of the next 2 sc - 67 sc. Join. Attach Floral. Fasten off Muslin.
Rnd 4: Ch 1, sc in same space as joining, work 2 sc in each of the next 3 sc, sc in each of the next 11 sc, skip next 7 sc, sc in each of the next 11 sc, work 2 sc in each of the next 5 sc. Sc in each of the next 17 sc, work 3 sc in next sc, sc in each of the next 17 sc - 78 stitches
Rnd 5: Ch 1, sc in each of the next 2 sc, work 2 sc in each of the next 3 sc, sc in each of the next 11 sc, decrease over next 2 sc. Sc in each of the next 11 sc, work 2 sc in each of the next 3 sc, sc in each of the next 23 sc, work 3 sc in next 2 sc, sc in each of the next 20 sc - 84 sc. Join. Attach Cranberry. Fasten off Floral.
Rnd 6: Ch 1, sc in same space as joining, work 2 sc in each of the next 2 sc, sc in each of the next 16 sc, decrease over next 2 sc. Sc in each of the next 16 sc, work 2 sc in each of the next 3 sc, sc in each of the next 21 sc, work 3 sc in next 2 sc, sc in each of the next 20 sc - 90 sc. Join. Attach Floral. Fasten off Cranberry.
Rnd 7: Ch 1, sc in each of the 2 sc, work 2 sc in each of the next 2 sc, sc in each of the next 2 sc, work 2 sc in next sc. Sc

in each of the next 14 sc, skip next sc, sc in each of the next 14 sc, work 2 sc in next sc, sc in each of the next 2 sc, work 2 sc in next 2 sc, sc in each of the next 26 sc. Work 3 sc in next sc, sc in each of the next 23 sc - 98 sc. Join.
Rnd 8: Ch 1, sc in each of the 6 sc, work 2 sc in each of the next 2 sc, sc in each of the next 14 sc, decrease over next 2 sc. Sc in each of the next 14 sc, work 2 sc in next sc, sc in each of the next 2 sc, work 2 sc in each of the next 2 sc, sc in each of the next 32 sc, work 3 sc in next sc, sc in each of the next 25 sc - 103 sc. Join.
Rnd 9: Ch 1, sc in same space as joining, sc in each of the next 3 sc, work 2 sc in next sc, sc in each of the next 20 sc, skip next sc. Sc in each of the next 20 sc, work 2 sc in next sc, sc in each of the next 3 sc, work 2 sc in next sc, sc in each of the next 26 sc, work 3 sc in next sc, sc in each of the next 26 sc - 108 sc. Join. Fasten off Floral. Weave in end.

Twisted Loop Border: With right side of rug facing, hold rug upside down and attach Cranberry in 3rd sc of tip (at left of center sc of group). *Hold loop on hook with finger to keep it from slipping off hook. Turn hook clockwise one complete turn. Ch 7. Carefully remove loop from hook and hold loop with other hand. Do not let chain untwist. Skip 2 sc. Insert hook from right side of rug to pull up loop from back, sl st. Repeat from * around - 36 loops. Join with sl st in last sc. Fasten off. Weave in end.

THE MOSAIC PROJECT BOOK

ORIENTAL STYLE

DONNA REEVES

Mosaic design has often been described as 'painting by numbers' and, however basic a description this might be, it does provide a clue to this art form's key attraction – its accessibility. Mosaics are simply the creation of patterns and pictures from pieces of stone, ceramics, porcelain or glass . . . what could be simpler?

The designs range from very simple to very detailed – both can be beautiful. Start with straightforward designs and, as you gain in confidence, move onto more ambitious projects. Experiment with different materials and designs. You will soon discover why mosaics have existed as an art form for over 2,000 years – some even date the earliest examples of mosaics back to Ancient Mesopotamia in around 3,000 BC. The combination of their decorative and functional attributes ensured the future of mosaics as a versatile and durable art form that will always have an ageless appeal. All you need to enjoy mosaic design is time, patience and imagination.

MATERIALS

Tesserae (which comes from the Latin word for 'square' and Greek word for 'four') is the name of the pieces used to make mosaics. They come in all manner of shapes and sizes and are supplied on sheets or loose. When storing tesserae, you need to make them easily identifiable, so glass or transparent containers are ideal for loose cubes and clearly labelled boxes work well for flat sheets. All adhesives, cements and additives are best stored in a dry, cool place.

Below is a list of the main materials used in mosaic design. However, there are no rules and mosaicists can use any number of other materials including glass beads, buttons, coins, shells, slate, semi-precious stones and broken household china.

Marble tesserae Available in a natural palette of colours, marble tesserae have either polished or unpolished finishes: the former gives a smooth elegant finish whereas the latter has a more rustic look. Cut marble using a hammer and hardie (bolster blade; see page 4) and protect with a sealant. Pieces are commonly 1.5 x 1.5cm (⅝ x ⅝in).

Vitreous glass Available in a range of colours and palettes, these are relatively cheap and resistant to heat and frost making them ideal for both interior and exterior use. Cut glass using mosaic nippers (see page 4). They are usually supplied in single colour sheets of 2 x 2cm (¾ x ¾in) or loose in mixed bags.

Porcelain These are usually supplied unglazed and are available in a wide range of shades. Suited to internal and external application, they offer excellent 'slip'-resistant properties even when wet. Use mosaic nippers for cutting (see page 4) and follow the advice of your tile supplier with regard to sealants.

Ceramic These are similar to porcelain tesserae except that they are usually glazed.

Smalti These are made from glass, which are prepared and cut into rectangular strips and then into rectangular tesserae. Smalti reflect light beautifully due to irregularities caused by hand-cut glass surfaces. Sold by the 500g (1lb) or 1kg (2lbs) usually in pieces of 1 x 1.5cm (½ x ⅝in), smalti are quite expensive but worth every penny! They can be used internally and externally because they are heat and frost proof. Use a hammer and hardie (bolster blade) to cut smalti.

Gold or silver leaf These tesserae are made when a thin layer of 24-carat gold, or silver, is hammered onto a coloured glass backing and covered with a film of veneer glass. These are then hand cut into tesserae, which can lead to irregularities in sizes and shapes. Either plain or rippled, these should be used sparingly for decorative purposes only because the silver or gold breaks down in excessive conditions, such as extreme heat and frost.

Pebbles or stones Available in a variety of colours, sizes and textures, granite and hard stones are recommended for durability and can be used internally and externally.

Household ceramic tiles These come in a wonderful range of colours and sizes, and are very cheap, which makes experimental cutting affordable. Always check the durability of tiles because certain types are prone to cracking under extreme conditions.

Glass and mirror Use these to add a reflective quality to your mosaics. They are available in large panels from glass shops and some tile suppliers, and should be cut very carefully with a glass cutter.

BASIC TOOLS AND TECHNIQUES

The basic mosaicist tool kit is very simple and you may already have most of this equipment around your home. If not, visit a hardware store, builders' merchant or tile supplier (see page 32).

1. Hardie Sometimes called a bolster blade, this is used with a hammer for cutting marble and smalti. The hardie is a small metal block with an anvil-shaped edge, which can either be embedded in concrete in a flower pot or in an upright log.

2. Hammer This is curved on one edge and tipped with tungsten carbide. There are various weights – you should find one that is comfortable for you but that is in proportion with the hardie (bolster blade).

3. Mouth and nose filter masks Wear these when cutting tesserae, mixing grout and cement or using strong smelling solvents.

4. Mosaic nippers These are used to cut vitreous glass, porcelain and ceramic tesserae. The cutting edge is tipped with tungsten carbide for durability. Buy nippers with spring action handles to make cutting less arduous.

5. Tile cutters These cutters carve through tiles in a two-step process. On one part of the cutters is a small wheel or blade and on the other, a flat edge known as the snapper. First the tile is scored with the blade and then 'snapped' with the flat edge.

6. Electric drill This is used for fixing mosaic projects. Buy a selection of rawl plugs and screws and invest in a countersink bit, which hides screw heads. A jigsaw is also a useful tool for delicate, intricate cutting.

7. Gummed brown paper or brown paper One side of the former type is gummed, which, when damp, will bond tesserae temporarily making it ideal for the indirect method (see page 7). If you use brown paper, apply gum glue to the shiny side.

8. Wood Used as a base material or support, the type of wood you use will depend on the weight and size of your mosaic, and whether it will be featured indoors or outside. Always prime before use.

9. Paintbrush/glue spreaders These are to paint and prime surfaces.

10. Polyvinyl acetate (PVA) glue This is excellent for priming or preparing surfaces.

11. Tape measure/ruler Measuring tools.

12. Spirit level This has a liquid measure and, when the bubble is central, the surface measured is straight. Check surfaces are straight before mosaicing directly onto the walls.

13. Safety glasses Wear these when cutting tesserae as slivers can damage your eyes.

14. Scissors Cutting tool for paper/card.

15. Gum glue This is a water-based adhesive. It is normally used with brown paper in the indirect method (see page 7).

16. Tweezers These are wonderful for picking up small tesserae and placing them in position or for pricking out unwanted pieces.

17. Bradawl This makes an excellent 'prodder' or pricking-out implement, which removes unwanted cement and mosaics.

18. Stanley knife Cutting tool for paper/card.

19. String Useful for creating large circles.

20. Masking tape This is not as sticky as adhesive tape and so is ideal for attaching the template to tracing paper temporarily.

21. Graph paper and sketch pad These are especially useful during the design stages.

22. Markers, pens and pencils Use markers to draw your design on the base of the mosaic. Pens and pencils are essential throughout.

SAFETY ADVICE

When cutting:
▶ wear surgical gloves, safety glasses, mouth and nose filters
▶ wear closed-toe shoes
▶ lay dust sheets if working indoors

When applying adhesives, grouts or sealants:
▶ follow manufacturers' instructions
▶ wear surgical or rubber gloves
▶ work in well-ventilated areas and, if necessary, use mouth and nose filters
▶ wear an apron or overalls
▶ lay dust sheets

When drilling:
▶ always unplug when changing bits
▶ wear safety glasses

CUTTING AND SCORING

MOSAIC NIPPERS: These are used to cut vitreous glass and porcelain tesserae. Hold the nippers in one hand and the tesserae in the other. Before cutting, get used to handling the nippers, which should be held towards the bottom of the handles. Place the tesserae face up in between the cutting edges of the nippers and then apply firm pressure.

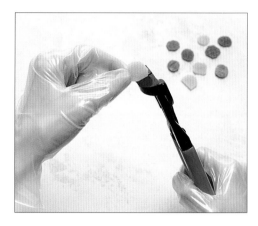

Cutting in half Place the tessera halfway into the mosaic nippers. Squeeze the handles firmly and the tessera will break in half. If you need quarters, take half a tessera and repeat the procedure. The quarters can also be cut in half to create smaller tesserae that are ideal for outlining.

Cutting diagonals Place the tessera diagonally into the cutting edges of the nippers. Apply pressure and the piece should cut forming two triangles.

Cutting curves or circles This shape is slightly more fiddly to perfect than halves or diagonals, but can be achieved if you nip off each of the corners of the tessera. Then slowly 'nibble' all the way around the tile in order to produce a smooth round circular or oval shape.

HAMMER AND HARDIE (BOLSTER BLADE): Used to cut smalti and marble, this is similar to a tool used by the Romans. Make sure that your cutting hand is not restricted and be patient – perfect results take time.

TILE CUTTERS: These are useful if you want to cut ceramic tiles that measure more than 2.5cm square (1in square) and are ideal if you are using spare tiles left over from the bathroom or kitchen. They have a dual function: first, the cutter blade scores a line along the tile and then the snappers break it. For ceramic squares, cut strips and then score and snap them into squares. You can get larger cutters or cutting machines for cutting thicker tougher tiles.

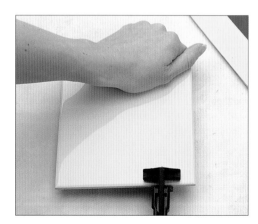

Hammer and hardie (bolster blade) Position the tessera with your thumb and finger over the blade of the hardie where you want the cut to be. Bring the hammer down lightly and firmly onto the centre of the tessera. Avoid inhaling dust by standing back as you cut.

Scoring tiles In order to produce a scored line on your ceramic tile, place a metal rule in the exact position that you want the desired cutting line. Then run the tile cutter's blade along the metal rule applying even pressure as you go.

Snapping tiles Put the tile cutter's mouth over the centre of the scored line. Use your other hand to take the pressure away from the cut. Apply firm pressure to the cutters until you hear a 'snapping' noise when the tile is cut.

ADHESIVES, GROUTS AND TOOLS

There are different types of adhesives and grouts available but it is important that you choose the correct one for your project's requirements.

1. Polyvinyl acetate (PVA) glue (illustrated on page 3) A white glue that comes in two forms: water soluble and non-water soluble. The former can be used in the indirect method (see page 6). Also used to prime surfaces.

2. Gum glue (illustrated on page 3) This is usually water soluble and is used for the indirect method (see page 6).

3. Cement-based adhesives These are available in powder, ready-mixed or rapid setting forms. Using an additive will allow more movement and flexibility.

4. Mortar mix (not illustrated) Made from sand, cement and water, this is ideal for making an exterior floor mosaic. The ratio is generally 3:1, sharp sand to cement.

5. Grout Used to fill the gaps between the tesserae, this comes in ready-mixed or powder form and a variety of colours. Illustrated here is the cement-based powder form. Ready-made products are also available but they tend to leave a residue behind.

6. Epoxy Grout (not illustrated) This is a two-part resin-based grout, which creates a waterproof barrier.

7. Paint Scraper This is used to mix and apply small amounts of adhesive and grout.

8. Notched trowel This is used for laying the cement and it has a serrated or notched edge that combs the bed of cement, ensuring an even layer and creating a good key. A 3mm (⅛in) notched trowel is recommended for mosaics as it creates a smaller grooved bed.

9. Trowel Use a pointed-head trowel for applying cement in awkward areas, and for measuring and mixing adhesive and grouts.

10. Margin trowel Square-headed trowel.

11. Palette knives Available in different shaped heads, this is a flexible tool that is

great for applying adhesive or grout in small areas and to smooth and remove excess.

12. Protective gloves Use rubber gloves when cleaning and grouting and surgical gloves when applying adhesive and cutting tesserae.

13. Grout float Used for applying grout, especially on larger projects, it also removes grout residue. Use a squeegee as an alternative.

14. Cloth Use for polishing grout residue.

15. Tiler's sponge Ideal for removing grout and cleaning. Use the sponge in circular movements to ensure an even coverage.

16. Sealants A wide variety of sealants are available – seek advice from a tile supplier for the product most suited to your project.

17. Additive for adhesive This is used with powdered adhesive and allows more natural movement. It is especially important when working on wood and floorboards.

18. Additive for grout This is used with the powdered grout and allows for flexibility. Read the label for safety advice.

19. Measuring jug This is used when measuring ratios of water, grout and glue.

MIXING CEMENT AND GROUT

Measuring ingredients Follow the manufacturers' instructions with regard to quantities and ratios of ingredients – you can use various measuring devices, such as one full trowel or one full measuring jug to represent one unit of material.

Adding water Pour the ingredients into a clean bucket. Slowly add water and additive, and mix with a trowel.

Smoothing the mixture Using a small trowel, mix the ingredients thoroughly. The texture should be quite smooth and free of lumps, neither too runny nor too thick.

DIRECT MOSAIC-LAYING METHOD

 Employing this method means that you apply the tesserae 'directly' in situ; that is, face up and one at a time straight onto the adhesive. The benefit of this technique is that you can see the work progress piece by piece. It is used in three-dimensional projects, on uneven surfaces, or in murals and splashbacks. The direct method is not recommended for flat surfaces as the results may be irregular.

1 Using abrasive paper and a block, remove the rough edges from the chosen base – here, a piece of wood. Run over the face of the base to create a good key.

2 Paint the front and side edges with one coat of PVA glue to prime the surface. Make sure you clean your brush immediately after use, or it will become stiff.

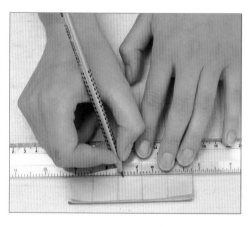

3 While waiting for the glue to dry, prepare the adhesive and soak the mosaic pieces to free them from the brown paper backing. Once the PVA has dried completely, draw on your design with a pencil or marker pen.

4 Spread a small amount of adhesive onto the board and position the mosaic piece by piece, following your pencil design. Leave to dry for 24 hours. Wear gloves to protect your hands from the adhesive.

5 Clean your panel with a damp sponge then prick out excess cement with a bradawl or similar tool so that it will not show through the grout. If using marble tesserae, apply a protective coating.

6 Put on rubber gloves and mix a quantity of grout (see page 5). For small projects use a paint scraper, as shown, to squeeze the grout into the gaps between the tiles. Use a grout float or squeegee for larger projects.

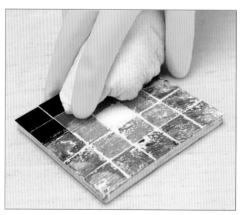

7 After completely grouting the finished piece, remove the excess grout using a clean, damp sponge. Repeat this process several times and rinse your sponge regularly to keep it clean and avoid smearing.

8 Use a cloth to polish the surface, removing any residue. Leave the grout to dry for 24 hours and then apply a sealant to marble or porcelain tiles with a paintbrush or cloth, to protect them from staining.

INDIRECT MOSAIC-LAYING METHOD

 This method is 'indirect' in the sense that you first lay out the mosaic on gummed brown paper, before pressing the entire finished design onto your chosen base. The indirect method is best used for larger projects, such as floors, so you can achieve a uniform flat surface and work in sections at a time. It is also better for laying mosaic in areas that are not easily accessible.

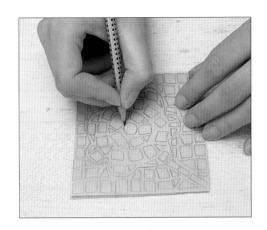

1 Draw your design and then trace onto tracing paper. Turn it over and transfer onto gummed paper (sticky side up) or brown paper, showing the design in reverse.

2 Cut the tesserae with nippers, then stick them in position face down on the paper. For gummed paper use water for bonding; for brown paper use a water-soluble glue.

3 Remove any rough edges, then prime your surface with PVA glue using a paintbrush. Prepare your adhesive-based cement (see page 5) and apply it to the base using a paint scraper. Wear gloves to protect your hands.

4 Drag a notched trowel at a 45-degree angle towards you in one sweeping action. This creates a grooved surface in the adhesive, which provides a good key in which the tesserae can bond.

5 Carefully lift the mosaic and line its top edge with the top of the wood. Slowly lower the mosaic onto the adhesive bed. Smooth and press the tesserae with your hands. Leave to dry for 24 hours.

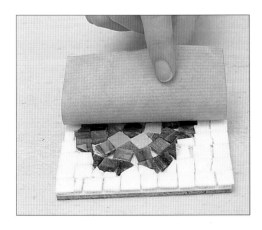

6 Moisten the paper with a wet sponge and peel it off to reveal the design. If any tesserae are attached to the paper, stick them down again with more adhesive and leave to dry. Prick out excess cement with a bradawl.

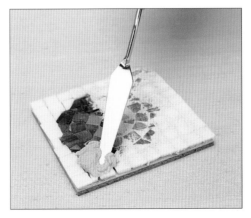

7 Wearing rubber gloves, prepare and apply the grout, pushing it into the gaps. Remove any excess with a damp sponge, rinsing the sponge frequently to avoid simply smearing rather than removing the grout.

8 Polish the mosaic with a cloth to remove the fine layer of grout residue. Leave to dry for 24 hours and then polish once again. For marble mosaics you will need to apply a coat of sealant using a cloth or paintbrush.

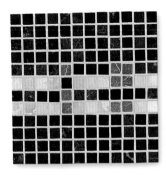

Zen Garden Wall Tiles

Create a Zen feel in your garden by adding these simple, yet stylish, garden tiles to any wall. Their refined design is a great backdrop for relaxation and calm. In the Chinese and Japanese school of Mahayana Buddhism, it is believed enlightenment can be attained through the practice of reflection and meditation. Add the tiles to a peaceful corner of your garden to complement a relaxed seating area with a screen of oriental bamboo. This is an ideal first project for beginners as there is no cutting involved. Our colour scheme features black, cream, green, terracotta and white with grey vein marble mosaic. The marble has been polished to add to the elegant look. Feel free to experiment and create your own tiles by using different mosaic colours or a different design.

TOOLS AND MATERIALS

PVA glue and paintbrush
Surgical and rubber gloves
Scissors
Bradawl or prodding tool
6 pieces of marine plywood cut to
20cm (8in) long x 20cm (8in) wide
x 2cm (¾in) depth
Sponge
White powder grout and additive
Notched trowel – 3mm (⅛in)
Trowel
Cloth
Safety goggles and mask
Marble protector
Colour enhancer
Marble impregnator
Stanley knife
Abrasive paper and block
White powder adhesive and
additive
Two buckets for mixing
Grouting float
Paintbrush and white emulsion (or
a colour of your choice)
Tracing paper
Clear yacht varnish

POLISHED MARBLE TESSERAE

Polished Marble Tesserae size =
1.5 x 1.5cm (⅝ x ⅝in)

Black = *Nero Marquina (RH)*
White with grey flecks = *Bianco
Cararra (RH)*
Green = *Verde Alpi (RH)*
Terracotta = *Rosso Verona (RH)*
Cream = *Botticino (RH)*
(See page 32 for list of suppliers)

USING THE TEMPLATE

Detach the template at the back of the book. Turn the tracing paper over and trace the outline on the reverse in pencil. Turn it back over and place it on top of the marine plywood. Trace over the front, transferring your design onto the board, ready to use the direct method as explained on page 6. There are four separate designs and two plain designs that do not need a template.

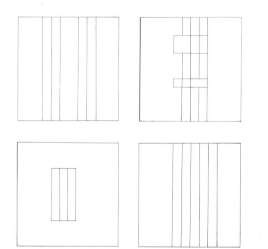

1 Remove the rough edges from all six marine ply boards, using abrasive paper and block. Then clean away the dust with a dry cloth. Apply one coat of PVA adhesive to the top and edges of the board and leave it to dry.

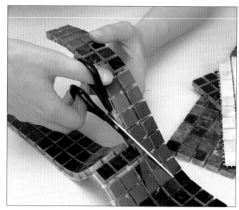

2 Leave the plastic or brown paper backing on which the mosaics are supplied and cut the sheet with scissors. Remove the template from the back of the book and place the tesserae into the correct position, one wall tile at a time.

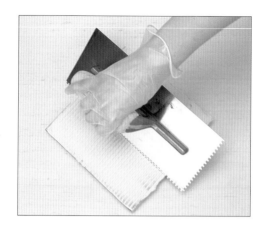

3 Mix some adhesive and apply it onto the wood with a trowel and smooth down. Then drag the notched trowel back towards you at a 45 degree angle making grooves. The grooves will provide a good key in which the tesserae can bond.

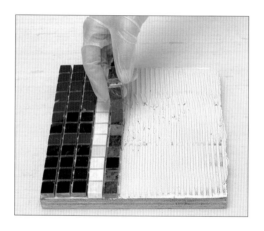

4 Transfer the marble line by line into the adhesive. Work on one tile at a time so the adhesive doesn't dry out. You may need to use a ruler to keep the mosaic running in straight lines.

5 Once all six tiles are completed leave them to dry for 24 hours. Clean with a damp sponge and remove excess adhesive with a bradawl or similar tool.

6 Apply a marble impregnator and protector with a clean paintbrush (read the manufacturer's instructions for drying time). Mix enough white powder grout for 6 tiles and apply using the grouting float. Push the grout firmly into the spaces between the tesserae. Wipe away the excess grout with a damp sponge. Leave to dry for 24 hours.

7 Clean the tiles with a dry cloth to remove grout residue. Once the grout has dried, paint the edges and backs of the tiles a colour of your choice (white was used for our tiles). Then varnish them for extra protection against all weather conditions.

8 Apply a marble 'colour enhancer' with a cloth and leave to dry. As the name suggests, this will bring out the colour of the marble and protect it. If you have any queries it is best to seek advice from your marble suppliers.

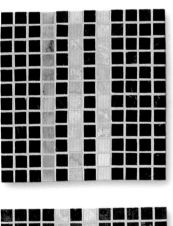

HINTS AND TIPS

▶ If you are experimenting with different mosaic colours or designs, make sure the type of mosaic you choose is suitable for exterior use, and make sure the board is the correct size to fit all the tiles on.

▶ Ask advice from a hardware shop about the best method of fixing them to the garden wall.

▶ Wash your paintbrush immediately after use to remove any PVA glue. Also wash adhesive and grouting tools after use.

▶ Marine ply is waterproof, but it is advised to apply PVA glue to the edges because when it is cut the exposed edges are not waterproof.

▶ Work on one tile at a time until you reach the grouting stage, which can be completed in one go.

▶ Before grouting, it is helpful to brush on a marble impregnator followed by a marble protector, available from most tile suppliers. These protect the marble from dirt and staining.

▶ Remove any adhesive that seeps over the side with a damp sponge.

▶ Read pages 3, 4 and 5 for advice on safety and mixing before starting this project.

INSPIRATIONAL IDEAS

These tiles could also be used as indoor wall hangings. You do not need to make all 6.

You could repeat the design and turn it into a beautiful floor pattern or kitchen splashback – obviously you would not need wood for this.

They could also be made into dinner place mats and you could produce smaller versions for drinks coasters.

Chinese Peony Mirror

TOOLS AND MATERIALS

Abrasive paper and block
Rubber and surgical gloves
Pencil and ruler
Wood cut to 80cm (31in) long x
60cm (23in) wide
Mirror cut to 60cm (23in) long x
20cm (8in) wide
Gum glue and brown paper
Grout float
Stanley knife and palette knife
PVA glue and paintbrush
Mosaic nippers
Safety goggles and mask
Powder adhesive and additive
Two buckets for mixing
Margin trowel
Notched trowel – 3mm (⅛in)
Sponge and cloth
Bradawl or prodding tool
White powder grout and additive
Blue paint (emulsion or acrylic)
and paintbrush
Tracing paper

VITREOUS GLASS MOSAICS

Glass Vitreous Tesserae size=
2 x 2cm (¾ x ¾in)
Baby pink – code = 20.18/1 (EU)
Lilac with gold vein – code =
20.95/4 (EU)
Candy pink – code = 20.4/5 (EU)
Blue with gold vein – code =
20.47/4 (EU)
Mint green with gold vein – code
= 20.39/4 (EU)
Misty white – code = 20.37/1 (EU)
(See page 32 for suppliers)

This elaborate, very feminine mirror has been created from vitreous glass mosaics. The palette is typically Chinese, combining lavish, vibrant colours that challenge the Western eye. The flowers featured are tree peonies symbolizing Spring, Riches, Honor, Love & Affection, Feminine Beauty, and Prosperity. Similar motifs can be seen in embroidery, textiles and Chinese ornamental art, for instance painted porcelain vases or bowls and paper cutting designs. This form of art, popular during the Ching Ming and earlier dynasties, was obscured by the style adopted during the 19th century, when the utilitarian, practical approach featured prominently and the decorative, more ornate styles were abandoned. It is quite a complicated design but with patience you'll recreate a beautiful, authentic-looking Chinese mirror which is worth the challenge.

USING THE TEMPLATE

This project involves both the direct and indirect method explained on pages 6 and 7. You only need to use the template for the two flower borders, where you will follow the indirect method. To do this, trace the template at the back of the book. Turn your tracing paper over and place onto a sheet of brown paper, shiny side up, then go over the outline of the design on the reverse in pencil. Turn it back over and place it on top of another sheet of brown paper, shiny side up. Trace over the lines once again, transferring your design onto the brown paper. This will produce the flower borders. Then follow the indirect method for laying your tesserae.

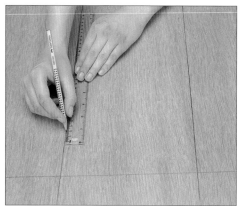

1 Cut the wood to 80cm (31in) length x 60cm (24in) width. Remove rough edges with abrasive paper and a block. Remove the sawdust then apply a layer of PVA glue with a paintbrush to the front and edges of the wood. Leave to dry.

2 Mark the two borders: bottom and top, 10cm (4in) width x 60cm (24in) length; the flower panels, 20cm (8in) width x 60cm (24in) length; and the area where the mirror will be should measure 20cm (8 in) width x 60cm (24in) length.

3 Mix some adhesive (see page 5). Apply using a trowel or margin trowel, but stay within your marked outline. Groove the bed using a notched trowel, then wash off adhesive. Position the mirror and firmly push it down with your hands.

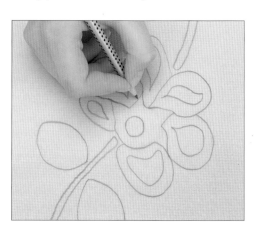

5 Trace the flower design onto the shiny side of the brown paper. Then reverse the flower design and trace once again, so you have 2 panels both in different directions. See the note about tracing the template on page 12.

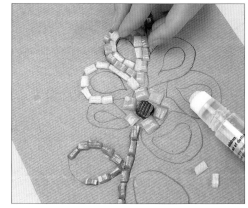

4 Start with the bottom and top borders of the mirror, following the direct method. Using a Stanley knife, cut a strip of blue mosaics 4 tesserae wide to fit the length. Position these directly (face down) into the adhesive bed. Line the blue mosaic to the edge of the board. Cut the candy pink mosaic and position it directly into the gap between the blue mosaic and the mirror. Repeat this procedure along the top and bottom of the mirror. Using a damp sponge, wet the paper backing and carefully peel it away from the tesserae.

6 Cut the mosaic with nippers (see page 3). Position onto the brown paper, using gum glue which is water soluble. Complete the detail of the flowers and then the background made up of random cut blue tesserae. Finish both panels.

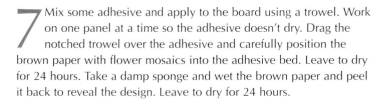

7 Mix some adhesive and apply to the board using a trowel. Work on one panel at a time so the adhesive doesn't dry. Drag the notched trowel over the adhesive and carefully position the brown paper with flower mosaics into the adhesive bed. Leave to dry for 24 hours. Take a damp sponge and wet the brown paper and peel it back to reveal the design. Leave to dry for 24 hours.

8 Prick out any dry excess adhesive, using a bradawl or similar tool, and clean the surface with a dry cloth. Then mix up some white powder grout and apply to the mosaic using a grout float. Clean with a damp sponge and polish. Leave to dry for 24 hours. Wash your bradawl and grout float immediately after use.

HINTS AND TIPS

▶ Read pages 3, 4 and 5 on safety, cutting and mixing before commencing this project.

▶ To free the tesserae from their backing, leave them to soak in warm water which will dissolve the glue; they will then be ready to use.

▶ Cut brown paper to the exact size needed for the flower borders before sticking on the tesserae. You will need enough brown paper for 2 borders.

▶ When grouting or using adhesive, fix some newspaper over the mirror with masking tape so as not to scratch the surface.

▶ When you have finished using the grouting float, adhesive trowel, buckets and paintbrush used for PVA, always wash them immediately.

▶ Paint the back and edges of the mirror with a blue emulsion or acrylic paint.

▶ For fixing, attach mirror glass plates into the back (in the wood) and then screw into the wall. You can buy mirror glass plates from any hardware shop.

INSPIRATIONAL IDEAS

This flower border could be repeated as a floor border for your bathroom or a skirting border in any other room. Choose complementary colours and remember to use a grout that matches your mosaic.

Oriental Screen

Screens have always played an important role in the oriental home, whether they have been designed to divide, conceal or protect. Traditionally they are beautifully decorated with recognisable symbols, like the crane here which was inspired by a Japanese screen painted in 1566. Cranes were commonly seen on objects d'art and 19th-century textiles. In Japan, cranes symbolize longevity and are also said to aid communication with the Divinities. The whiteness of the crane has been set on a jade green background, a familiar colour often used in oriental ornaments. Vitreous glass mosaics offer a wide colour range and thus texture and tone can be given to the crane's feathers with the various shades of white tesserae. To finish the screen we painted it black and varnished it to give it a lacquered feel.

USING THE TEMPLATE

Central panel: detach the template at the back of the book. Turn the tracing paper over and trace in pencil the outline of the bird and the outer edge, bordering the bird. Turn it back over and place it on top of the brown paper, shiny side up. Trace over the front, transferring your design onto the brown paper.

First and last panel: a template is not needed for these two panels as they consist of random cut pieces of jade mosaic with no pattern.

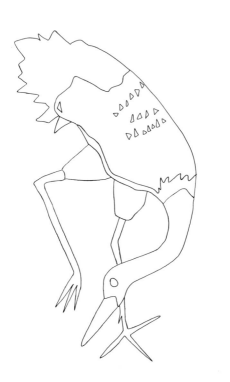

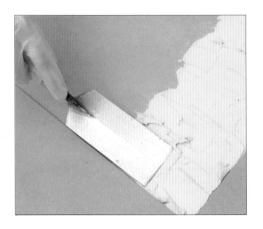

1 Remove any rough edges from the MDF with abrasive paper and a block. Then seal with PVA glue using a brush. Leave to dry. Wearing rubber gloves, mix some powder adhesive and apply to a portion of one panel with a margin trowel.

2 Groove the surface of the adhesive with a notched trowel. Cut the sage green mosaics in random shapes using mosaic nippers. Stick the tesserae into the adhesive bed, keeping the spaces between them equal. Repeat over first and last panels.

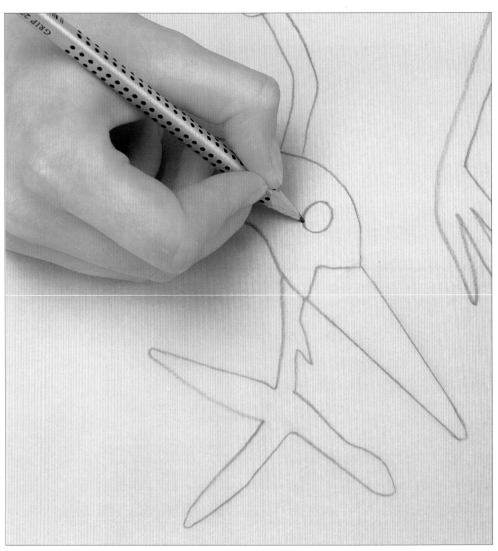

3 Central panel: follow the template instructions as explained on page 16. Trace the design onto some brown paper, shiny side up. It is a good idea to go over the pencil outline of the heron in black felt tip – this makes it easier to follow when you start sticking down the pieces. Secure the template to your base with masking tape while you are tracing your image, to help keep it in place. Once you have completed the design, cut all the coloured tesserae pieces you will need to complete the heron.

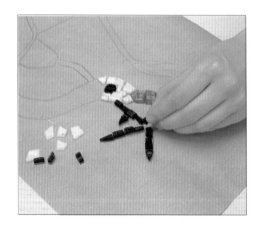

4 Central panel: start sticking the tesserae smooth side down onto the brown paper using gum glue, following the outline. Once the detail of the bird is complete, start on the background, using the jade mosaic. Leave to dry.

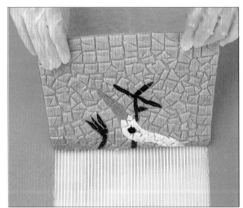

5 Central panel: mix some adhesive and apply it to the central panel then groove it with the notched trowel. Carefully place the mosaic on brown paper into the bed of adhesive. Leave it to dry for 24 hours.

6 Central panel: wet the brown paper using a damp sponge and gently peel it away. Use the abrasive side of the sponge to remove stubborn pieces of paper.

HINTS AND TIPS

▶ Paint the screen with black emulsion, wait for it to dry then varnish using clear yacht varnish.

▶ A carpenter made our screen and fixed the hinges. The positioning of the hinges determines the direction or angle of movement of the screen. You must decide how you want it to stand and inform your carpenter.

▶ It is advisable to cut the brown paper to the exact size and shape needed before sticking on your tesserae.

▶ To free the tesserae from their backing, leave them to soak in warm water which will dissolve the glue; they will then be ready to use.

7 Central, first and last panels: clean the mosaic with a sponge and prick out any unwanted lumps of adhesive with a bradawl or similar tool. Work on one panel at a time. Wash your panels with a damp sponge immediately after use.

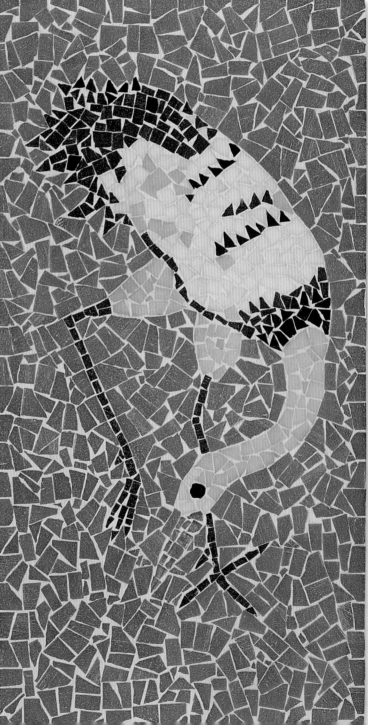

8 Central, first and last panels: mix some white grout and apply using a grout float. Remove excess grout with a damp sponge and polish with a dry cloth. Work on one panel at a time.

INSPIRATIONAL IDEAS

The bird design could be applied onto some marine ply, 54cm (21in) long x 28cm (11in) wide, and used as a decorative wall plaque in a garden.

Chinese Photo Album

T his decorative Chinese photo album would make an ideal gift or an excellent ornament. The simple colour scheme of white, black and gold creates a stylish look with a touch of wealth. The Chinese art symbol we have chosen means 'Riches', which could apply to the beautiful handmade album itself as well as the photos it contains with all their happy memories. To make the album really special you could add a leather strap for the tie and place some recycled paper inside, which you can either buy or make yourself. We chose a thick handmade paper with red rose petals sprinkled on a white background. Rice paper was cut and inserted between each sheet of handmade paper to protect the photographs, which can be attached with adhesive photo corners.

TOOLS AND MATERIALS

Electric drill with countersink bit
and screw-head bit (pilot hole)
2 pieces of 4mm (⅛in) plywood,
40cm (16in) long x 30cm (12in)
wide
Black emulsion paint
Clear yacht varnish
Paintbrush
Ruler and pencil
Glass tesserae 2 x 2cm (¾ x ¾in)
Brown paper for circular motif
Gum glue
Rubber and surgical gloves
Sponge and cloth
Tape measure
Leather strap
Recycled paper & rice paper
PVA glue
Mosaic nippers
Safety glasses and mask
White powder adhesive and
additive
2 buckets for mixing
Notched trowel – 3mm (¼in)
Trowel
Bradawl
White powder grout and additive
Hole punch
Tracing paper

VITREOUS GLASS MOSAICS

Glass Vitreous Tesserae size =
2 x 2cm (¾ x ¾in)

½ kilo (1lb) Gold leaf mosaic –
smooth surface(EU)
Charcoal – code = 20.65/2 (EU)
White – code = 20.37/1 (EU)
(See page 32 for key to suppliers)

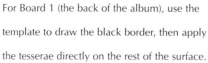

USING THE TEMPLATE

This project uses the direct and the indirect method. For Board 2, the front of the album, you should make the circular motif separately on brown paper. Detach the template, trace the back and then place onto the brown paper. Trace the lines again, transferring the design onto the brown paper. Once the black border has been laid you will apply tesserae directly to complete the background and no template is required for this area.

For Board 1 (the back of the album), use the template to draw the black border, then apply the tesserae directly on the rest of the surface.

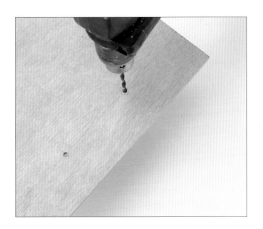

1 Drill two pilot holes through both boards at 5cm (2in) from the width of the board and 10cm (4in) away from the top/length. Remove the rough edges with abrasive paper and a block. Then apply PVA to the front on the boards. Leave to dry.

2 Paint the back of both boards using black emulsion paint. Leave to dry then varnish with clear yacht varnish. Cut the white mosaic in random shapes and the gold leaf in small oblong shapes, but leave the black mosaic on the sheets.

3 On the front of both boards, measure in 10.5cm (4in) from the outside edge. Mark a line at this level showing where the division between the white and black mosaic should lie.

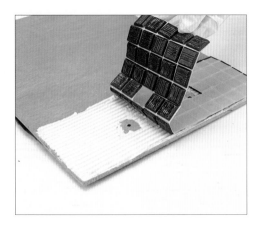

4 Boards One and Two: mix some adhesive and apply it where the black mosaic will be. Groove the surface with a notched trowel and place the mosaic smooth side up into the adhesive. Remove any tesserae that block the drilled holes.

5 Boards One and Two: remove any brown paper from the black tesserae by soaking them in warm water. Cut the mosaic to fit around the holes, making sure that you wear safety glasses when cutting. Place the mosaic into the adhesive.

6 Board Two (front of album): detach the template from the back of the book, trace the Chinese motif on the reverse side then trace the design onto some brown paper (see the instructions on page 20). Stick the tesserae (the gold leaf and white mosaic) smooth side down to the brown paper using gum glue.

7 Board Two (front of album): mix some adhesive and apply to the board. Groove the surface of the adhesive with a notched trowel. Position the Chinese motif on brown paper, paper side up, face down on top of the adhesive, making sure it is central. Then start sticking the white tesserae, smooth side up, directly into the adhesive. Fit the tesserae together like a jigsaw puzzle. If there are any gaps, you may need to cut exact pieces to fit. Leave to dry for 24 hours. On Board One (back of album), position white mosaics into the adhesive, smooth side up. Work around the symbol moving outwards until you have reached the edge of the album.

8 Board Two (front of album): take a damp sponge and wet the paper before peeling back to reveal the motif. Use a bradawl to prick out any unwanted adhesive.

9 Mix some grout and apply it to Boards One and Two using a grout float. Remove excess grout with a damp sponge and polish. Leave to dry for 24 hours.

INSPIRATIONAL IDEAS

This motif has such a beautiful appearance and meaning that it would make a wonderful wall plaque or a picture. You could find other Chinese symbols that appeal to you and create other mosaic projects.

HINTS AND TIPS

▶ It is advisable to cut the brown paper to the exact size and shape needed before sticking on your tesserae.

▶ To free the tesserae from their backing, leave them to soak in warm water which will dissolve the glue; they will then be ready to use.

▶ Always read the advice given on cutting, safety and mixing on pages 3, 4 and 5.

▶ After using PVA wash your paintbrush immediately with soapy water.

▶ Remove excess varnish from your paintbrush following the instructions given by manufacturers.

▶ You will need to cut the handmade and rice paper sheets to size and punch holes in them in the correct positions to match the outer shell of the album.

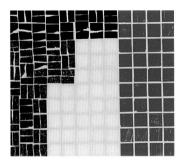

Japanese Sushi Table

T his beautiful, Japanese-inspired sushi table will look very stylish in any home. To create it, either use an existing table and re-invent it or make a new one from scratch. The geometric pattern on the tabletop reflects a simple, abstract Zen style that creates an interesting focal point to meals and a perfect backdrop to the delights of the Japanese delicacy of sushi – dainty packages of seaweed, rice and raw or cooked fish. The pattern consists mainly of vertical and horizontal rectangles and lines. The colours have been limited to black, white, grey and one of the primary colours, red. This would be a good choice as a project for a beginner, because it uses whole squares and gently introduces you to cutting the squares in half. If you are updating an existing table, make sure that you paint the legs with black paint and varnish to give a sleek lacquer finish.

TOOLS AND MATERIALS

Pencil and ruler
Spirit level
Abrasive paper and block
Surgical and rubber gloves
A table 90cm (35in) long
x 55cm (22in) wide
2 x 2cm (¾ x ¾in) glass tesserae
Mosaic nippers
Safety glasses and mask
PVA glue and paintbrush
Gum glue
Brown paper – enough to cover
60cm (24in) length x 40cm (16in)
width or the size of your table
Two buckets and a trowel
Bradawl or prodding tool
Notched trowel – 3mm (¼in)
Sponge and cloth
Grey powder adhesive & additive
White powder grout & additive
Clear yacht varnish
Black emulsion paint
Tracing paper

VITREOUS GLASS MOSAICS

Glass Vitreous Tesserae size =
2 x 2cm (¾ x ¾in)

Brown = 20.16/1 (EU)
Pillar Box Red = 20.80/3 (EU)
Pebble Grey = 20.86/2 (EU)
Misty White = 20.09/1 (EU)
Shiny Black = 20.77/3 (EU)
Charcoal = 20.65/2 (EU)
(See page 32 for suppliers)

USING THE TEMPLATE

Trace the template at the back of the book using your tracing paper. Turn the tracing paper over and trace the outline of the design on the reverse in pencil. Turn it back over and place it on top of some brown paper, which should be positioned shiny side up. Trace over the lines once again, transferring your design onto the brown paper. If you are using an existing table from home, as we have done, you may find that the template does not cover the full size of the tabletop so, using the direct method found on page 6, you can add a border around the template design, which is positioned in the centre.

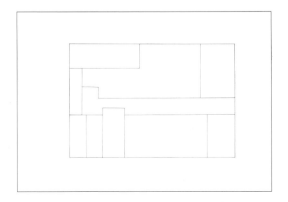

1 Using abrasive paper and block, sand the surface of your table top. Then prime it with PVA glue, using a paint brush. If you are updating an old table, ask your hardware shop which adhesive and primer will work best with the materials.

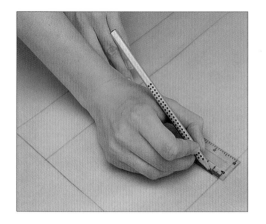

2 Trace the template design onto some brown paper, shiny side up. Then turn the paper over and mark a centre point, using a ruler and pencil, to ensure the template is in the centre when you stick it down onto the table.

3 Cut the pebble grey, shiny black and charcoal tesserae in half, using the mosaic nippers (see page 4 for an explanation of the cutting technique and page 3 for the safety advice). Leave the red and white mosaics whole. Then, using a damp sponge on sticky brown paper or gum glue on normal brown paper, stick the tesserae smooth side down into position. Complete the pattern and leave them to dry.

4 If your existing table top is larger than the template, mark a cross in the centre of the table. This should match the centre point drawn on the brown paper in Step 2. Draw in the full template oblong of 60cm (24in) length x 40cm (16in) width.

5 Mix some adhesive and using a trowel spread it into the marked shape. Groove the adhesive with a notched trowel and place the mosaics that you stuck to the brown paper into the adhesive, positioned with the rough side down.

6 If your table is larger than the template, using the direct method place the pebble grey mosaics, smooth side up, into some adhesive around the edges of the table to give it a neat border.

7 Wet the brown paper with a damp sponge and peel it off the mosaics. Any stubborn bits of paper can be removed by using the abrasive edge of the sponge. Then prick out any cement/adhesive that has seeped over the edge of the mosaic as this will show through the grout. The tool that is used for prodding in the photograph above is a bradawl. Wash the table with a damp sponge immediately after use.

8 Mix a quantity of grey grout and apply it using a grout float to push the grout into all the gaps. When you have finished, remove the excess grout with a damp sponge and polish your table with a dry cloth. Leave to dry for 24 hours.

HINTS AND TIPS

▶ It is advisable to cut the brown paper to the exact size and shape needed before sticking on your tesserae.

▶ To free the tesserae from their backing, leave them to soak in warm water; you'll find that this will dissolve the glue and they will then be ready to use.

▶ Read pages 3, 4 and 5 for information on cutting and mixing and advice on safety before commencing this project.

▶ If your table is larger than the template but you do not want to add a border to the design, you could extend the lines to the outer edge. You would either have to redraw the design to fit the table or wait for the template to dry on the adhesive peel-off paper and then extend the lines.

▶ If you are commissioning a new table for outdoors, use marine plywood for the top and galvanized steel for the base.

▶ Paint the table legs black and varnish them to give a lacquer effect.

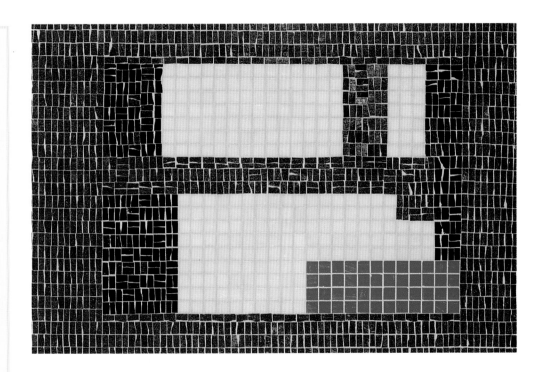

INSPIRATIONAL IDEAS

This versatile design could be used elsewhere, perhaps as a splashback for a kitchen wall or decorating the bottom of a Zen-style garden pond.

Plum Blossom Headboard

TOOLS AND MATERIALS

Fine liner pen (black)
Electric drill with countersink
and drill bit (for pilot hole)
Abrasive paper and block
Rubber and surgical gloves
Bradawl and palette knife
Grout float
Wood cut in circle of radius 21cm
(8in), diameter 42cm (16in)
10 screws of 2.5cm (1 inch)
2 planks cut to the size of your
bed – ours are 140cm (55in) long
Mosaic nippers
Safety goggles and mask
Notched trowel – 3mm (`in)
Two buckets for mixing
Powder adhesive and additive
Trowel
Sponge and cloth
Paintbrush and PVA glue
White powder grout and additive
Tracing paper and pencil
White gloss paint and paintbrush
White spirits

VITREOUS GLASS MOSAICS

Glass Vitreous Tesserae size =
2 x 2cm (¾ x ¾in)
Bright White – code = 20.10/1
(EU)
Bronze – code = 20.10/4 (EU)
Pink with gold vein – code =
20.11/4 (EU)
Lilac with gold vein – code =
20.95/4 (EU)
Mint green with gold vein –
code = 20.39/4 (EU)
Candy pink – code = 20.4/5 (EU)
(See page 32 for key to suppliers)

Futon beds have become popular accessories in the modern home. To update your futon, why not make a unique piece of art work – a decorative headboard. The mosaic features plum blossoms representing the return of spring. This design was inspired by an antique Chinese woman's informal robe, known as 'pei', with plum blossoms adorned on the front, back, sleeves and hem. The colours of the glass mosaic used are pretty pinks and purples that have gold veins running through them, not dissimilar to the coloured silks and threads seen in traditional Chinese robes and embroidery. The petals which are a major feature in the design are made from glass tesserae cut into circles. The branch of the plum blossoms is made by cutting tesserae in half, then quarters, then eighths, to create small tesserae for outlining.

USING THE TEMPLATE

Remove and detach the template found at the back of the book.

Turn the tracing paper over and trace the outline of the plum blossoms

on the reverse in pencil. Turn it back over and place into position

centred on the board. Trace over the front, transferring the design onto

the board. If the lines are too faint, go over them

with a fine (black) liner pen. Alternatively, if

you want to keep the template at the

back of the book, you should draw

the design on one side of the

tracing paper then turn it over to

trace through onto the back, using

a piece of scrap paper to shield your

work surface. Then trace the original

side onto your board to

transfer the design.

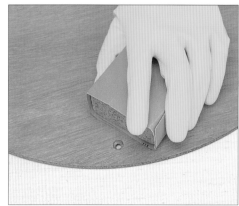

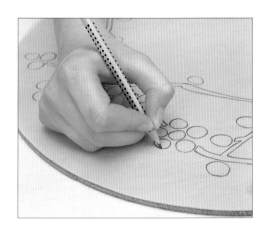

1 Cut the wood into a circle with a diameter of 42 cm (16in). Drill a pilot hole through the wood at the top and bottom leaving 2cm (¾in) from the edge. Use the countersink bit to go over the holes, which will hide the screw heads.

2 Using abrasive paper and block, remove the rough edges then apply PVA adhesive to the wood with a paintbrush. While you are waiting for it to dry, sand the two planks and paint them with white gloss paint.

3 Take the template from the back of the book and trace the design on the reverse side of the tracing paper. Then turn the tracing paper over and draw the tracing onto the wood. See page 28 for full instructions on using the template.

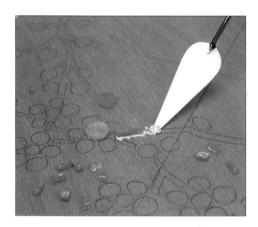

4 Cut your mosaic. Use the palette knife to apply a small amount of adhesive, working on the details first. The flowers are made from cut circles, and the branches are made by cutting the tesserae into eighths (see page 4 for instructions).

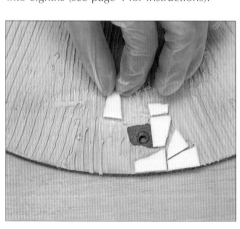

5 Once all the details are completed start on the background, which is made of randomly cut white mosaic. Make sure the fixing holes are free of adhesive.

6 Prick out the excess cement using a bradawl or a similar tool. Wipe the mosaic surface clean with a damp sponge and clean your bradawl after use. Once your mosaic is complete, leave it to dry for 24 hours. Make sure that you reserve some white mosaic pieces to cover over the fixing holes.

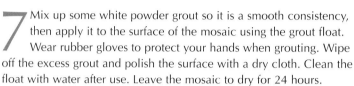

7 Mix up some white powder grout so it is a smooth consistency, then apply it to the surface of the mosaic using the grout float. Wear rubber gloves to protect your hands when grouting. Wipe off the excess grout and polish the surface with a dry cloth. Clean the float with water after use. Leave the mosaic to dry for 24 hours.

8 Fix the two planks onto the wall with screws. Centre the circle on top of the planks and make a pencil mark through each of the holes. Remove the panel and drill two pilot holes through the marks. Put the mosaic back into position and insert the screws. You may need a friend to help you hold the mosaic while you screw it into position. Mix some adhesive and stick the few remaining tesserae onto an adhesive bed. Allow 24 hours, then grout, clean and polish.

HINTS AND TIPS

▶ To free the tesserae from their backing leave them to soak in warm water, which will dissolve the glue; they will then be ready to use.

▶ Always read the safety tips and cutting and grouting advice given on pages 3, 4 and 5 before you begin this project.

▶ Whilst working on the mosaic, if you get any adhesive onto the tesserae, wipe them clean with a damp sponge.

▶ Wear surgical gloves when applying cement based adhesive.

▶ Wear rubber gloves when applying grout.

▶ Wash your paint brush with washing up liquid immediately after using PVA glue.

▶ Remove white gloss from your paintbrush immediately with white spirit.

INSPIRATIONAL IDEAS

If you want a soft headboard, add some stuffing, cover with material and staple it to the boards.

This would be easier to do before you fix the boards to the wall.

Or you could use this design as a decorative wall hanging instead of a headboard.

ACKNOWLEDGEMENTS

This book is dedicated to my husband, Nick Stringer, to remind him of our time spent in the orient and my naughty Nan who we left behind. Thanks to Abi Stringer, an excellent hand model and assistant, to Karen and Amy Milburn for typing the book, to Lauren Shear for being a perfectionist, to Lena Ikse Bergman for her calmness, to Natasha Martyn-Johns for spending long hours of discussion and to Cathy Layzell for posing and designing the layout of the book.

Thanks also to the following firms:

Edgar Udny & Co Ltd *[EU]*
314 Balham High Road
London SW17 7AA
Tel: 020 8767 8181
Fax: 020 8767 7709

Suppliers of vitreous glass, smalti, gold and silver leaf, as well as fixing materials and gummed brown paper. Mail order service available.

Reed Harris *[RH]*
Riverside House, 27 Carnwath Road
London SW6 3HR
Tel: 020 7736 7511
Fax: 020 7736 2988

Supplier of household tiles, porcelain and marble tesserae as well as sealants, tools, adhesives and grout. Mail order service available.

Paul Fricker Ltd
Well Park, Willeys Avenue
Exeter EX2 8BE
Tel: 01392 278636
Fax: 01392 410508

Specialists in glass tesserae and suppliers of all materials. Mail order service available.

Mosaics are sold nationwide by branches of **B&Q**, **Fired Earth** and **Hobby Craft**.

In Australia, materials are available from tiling specialists and major hardware stores.

About the author

Donna Reeves Mosaics offers a complete service, from design to installation. Commissioned works range from floors, borders, walls and splashbacks to wall hangings. Donna Reeves can be contacted at:
33A Kay Road, London, SW9 9DF
Fax: 020 7737 0761/Mobile: 0370 886 764

Published by Murdoch Books UK Ltd
First published in 2001

ISBN 1-85391-997 7
A catalogue record of this book is available from the British Library.
© Text, design, photography and illustrations Murdoch Books UK Ltd 2001.

Commissioning Editor: Natasha Martyn-Johns
Project Editor: Anna Nicholas
Designer: Cathy Layzell
Photographer: Lauren Shear
Stylist: Caroline Davis

CEO: Robert Oerton
Publisher: Catie Ziller
Publishing Manager: Fia Fornari
Production Manager: Lucy Byrne

Group General Manager: Mark Smith
Group CEO/Publisher: Anne Wilson

Colour separation by Colourscan, Singapore
Printed in Singapore by Imago

Murdoch Books UK Ltd
Ferry House, 51–57 Lacy Road,
Putney, London, SW15 1PR
Tel: +44 (0)20 8355 1480, Fax: +44 (0)20 8355 1499
Murdoch Books UK Ltd is a subsidiary of Murdoch Magazines Pty Ltd.

Murdoch Books®
GPO Box 1203
Sydney NSW 1045
Tel: +61 (0)2 9692 2347, Fax: +61 (0)2 9692 2559
Murdoch Books® is a trademark of Murdoch Magazines Pty Ltd.